Remember, that dreams have no expiration date. Never give up on your dreams, no matter your age. Let these stories inspire you to reach for the stars and believe in the magic within you.

Ana Teixeira

2024

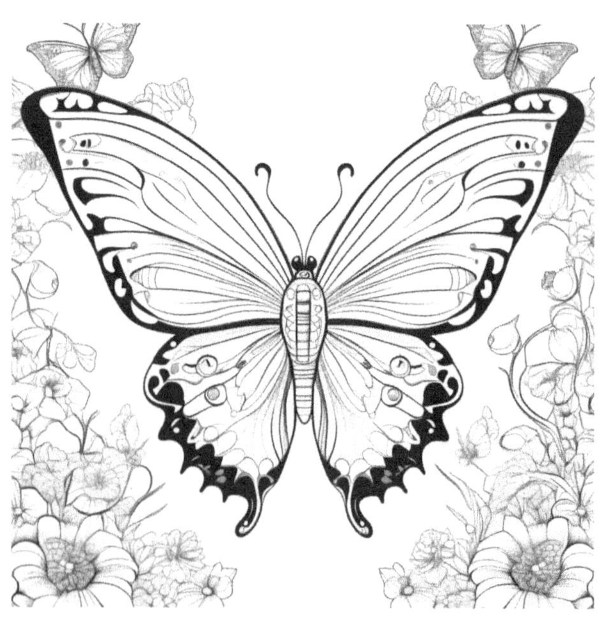

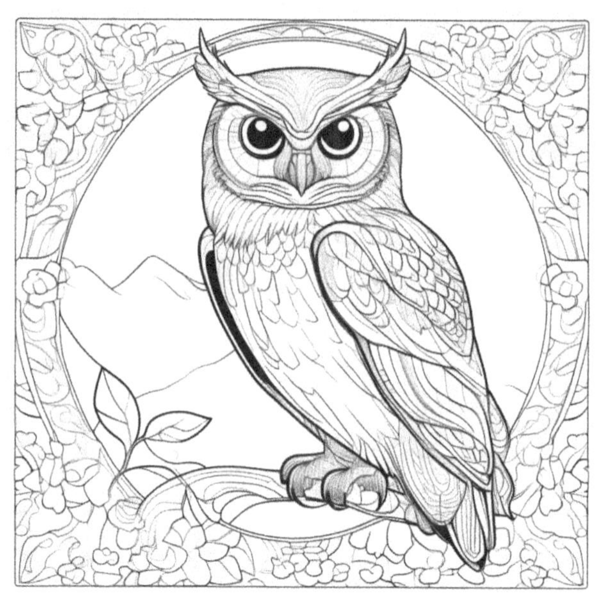

This Book Belongs to:

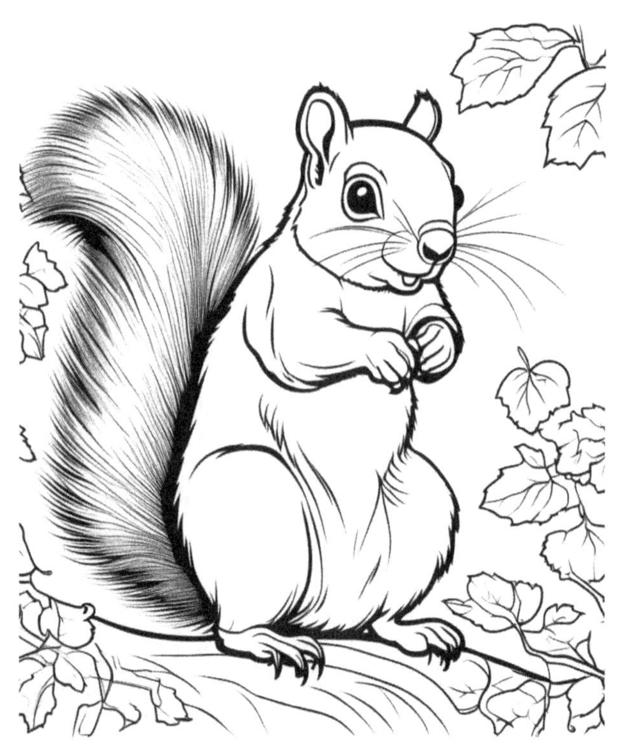

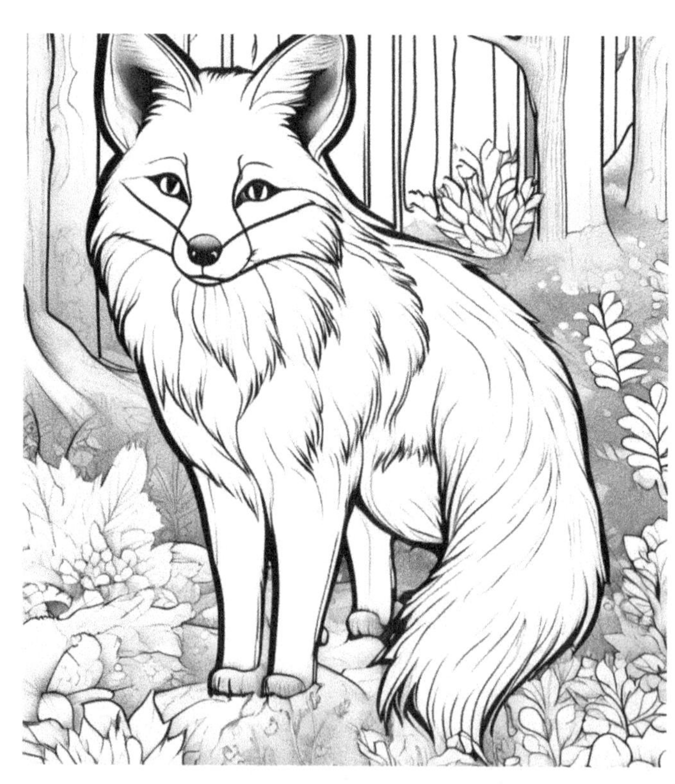

Get ready to join Lily and her faithful friend Scooby on a colorful adventure through the forest! As you turn each page, use your favourite colours to bring their journey to life. From vibrant trees to mystical creatures, your imagination will guide them through every twist and turn. Let's colour our way through this magical tale together!

Test Color Page

Once upon a time, in a cosy little village nestled at the edge of a vast forest, there lived a curious and kind-hearted girl named Lily, accompanied by her faithful companion, a dog named Scooby. Lily loved spending her days exploring the wonders of nature, from the towering trees to the babbling brooks that flowed through the forest.

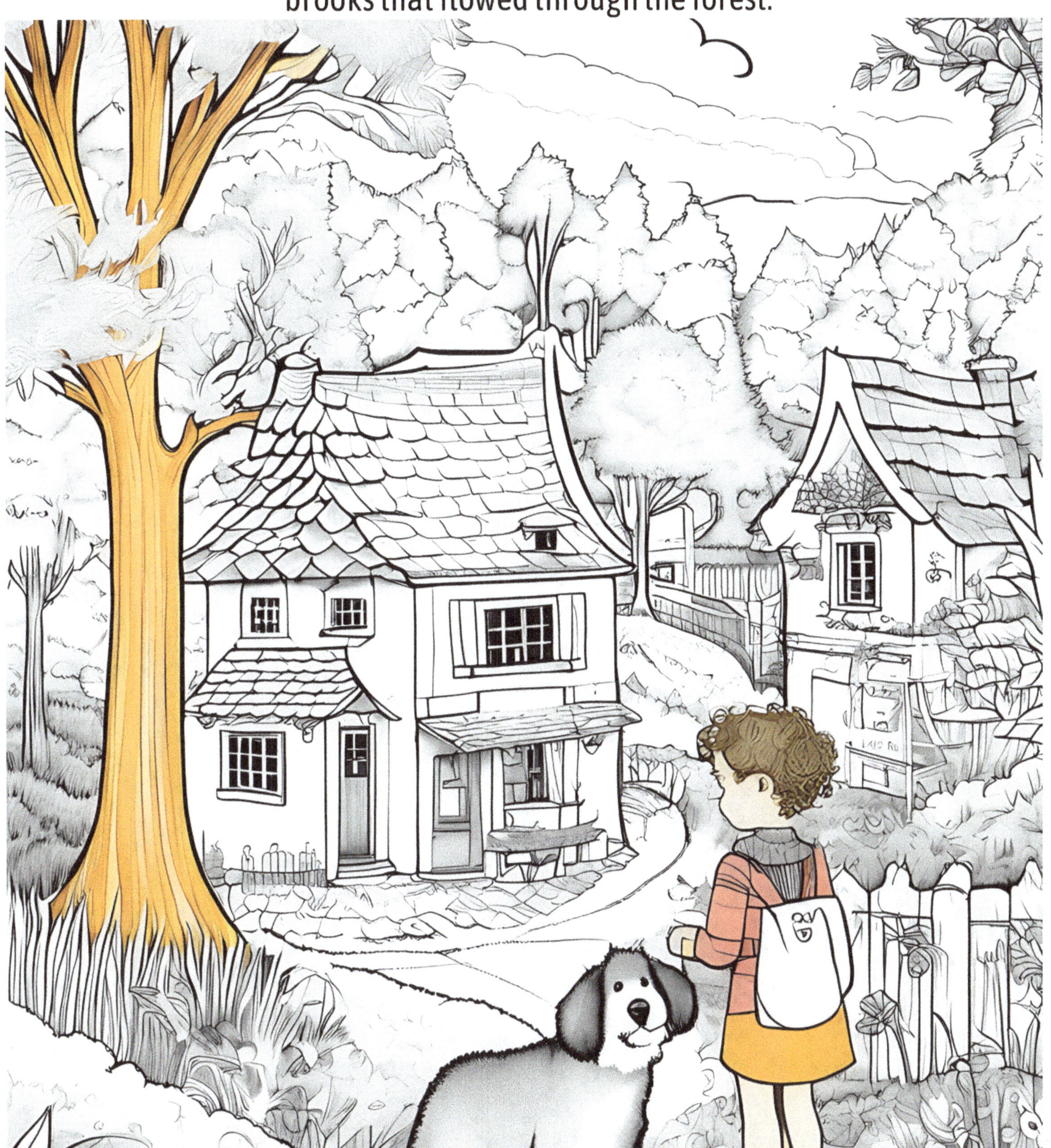

One sunny morning, as Lily set out on her daily adventure with her dog, she stumbled upon a wounded bird lying on the forest floor. With gentle hands, she scooped up the bird and nursed it back to health with love and care. From that day on, the bird, whom she named Feather, became her friend.

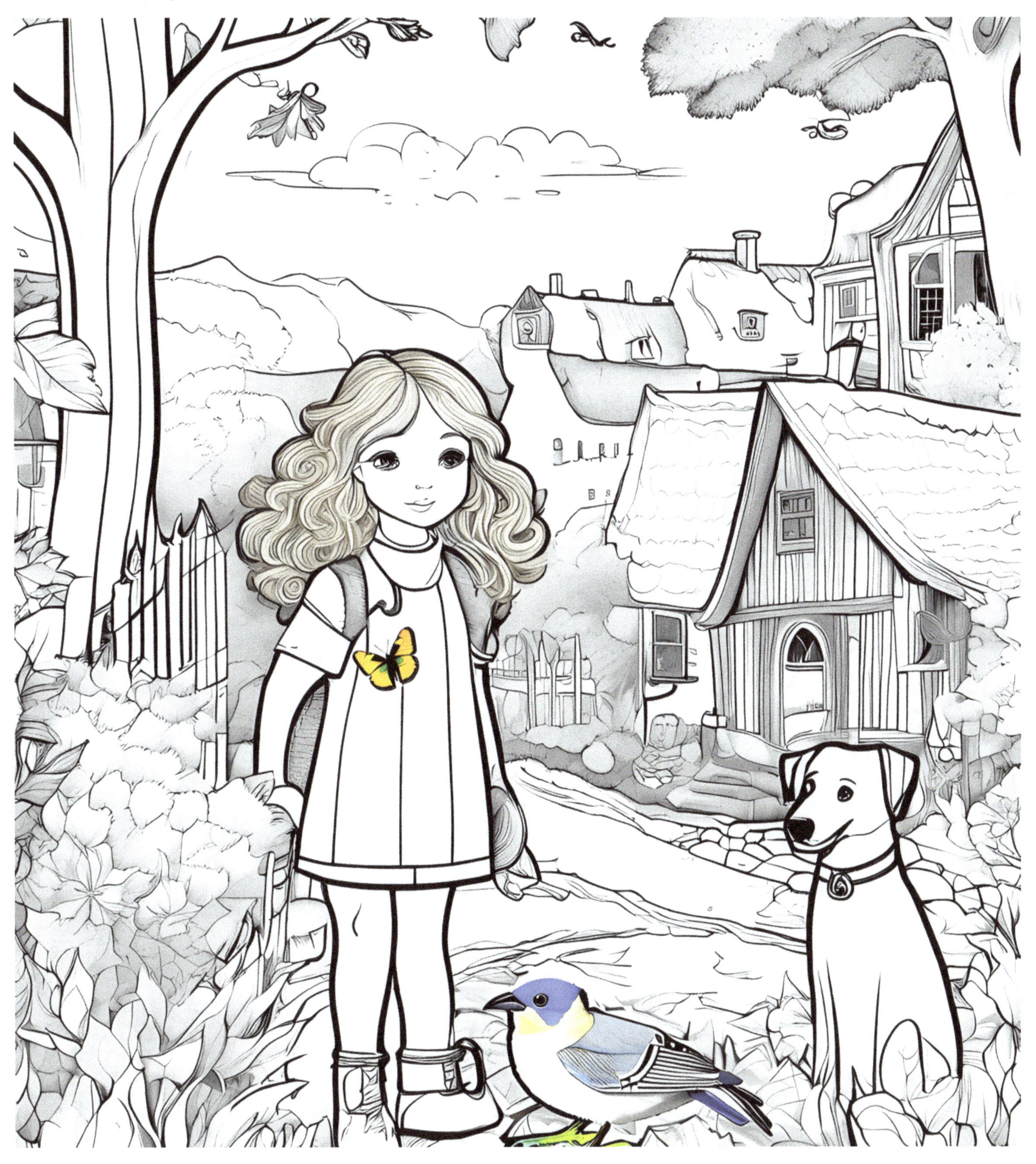

Together, Lily, Scooby and Feather embarked on many exciting journeys through the forest, meeting all sorts of wonderful creatures along the way. They befriended a wise old owl named Oliver, who taught them the secrets of the stars and the songs of the night.

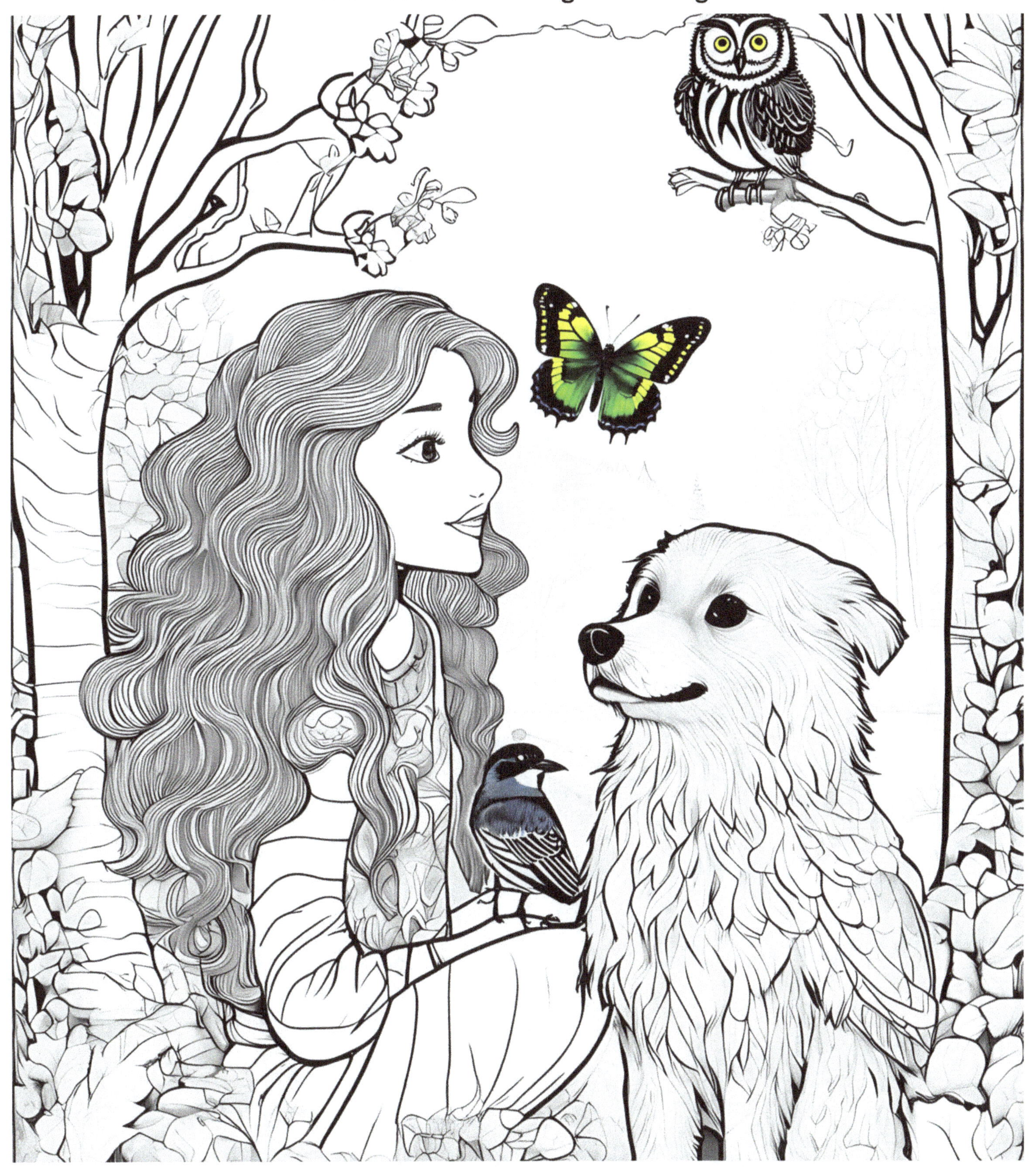

They also encountered a family of playful squirrels who showed them how to leap from branch to branch with grace and agility. And let's not forget about the mischievous foxes who taught them the importance of cleverness and resourcefulness.

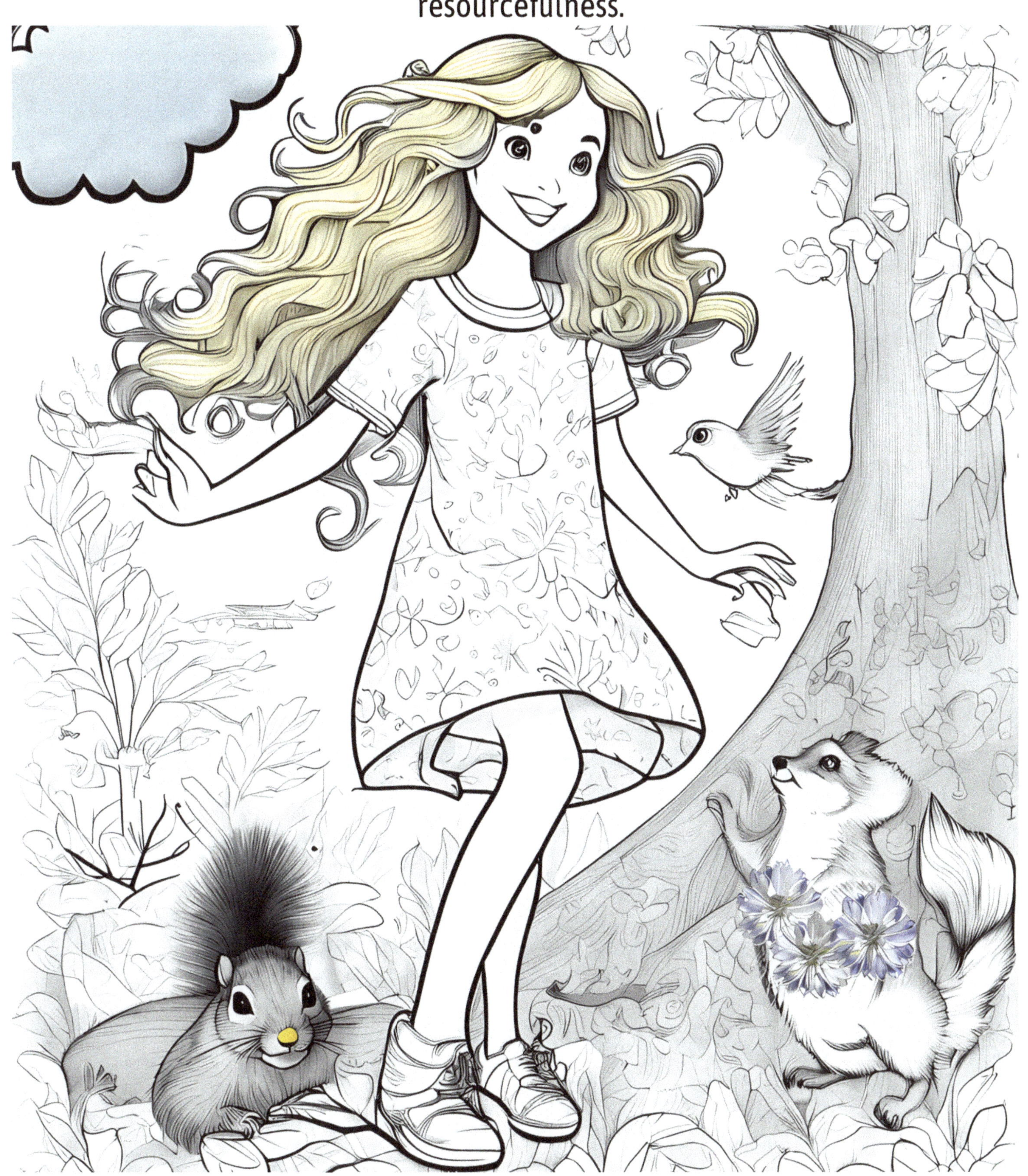

But as they explored deeper into the forest, Lily and her friends began to notice troubling signs. The once-lush greenery was starting to wither, and many of the animals were struggling to find food and shelter.

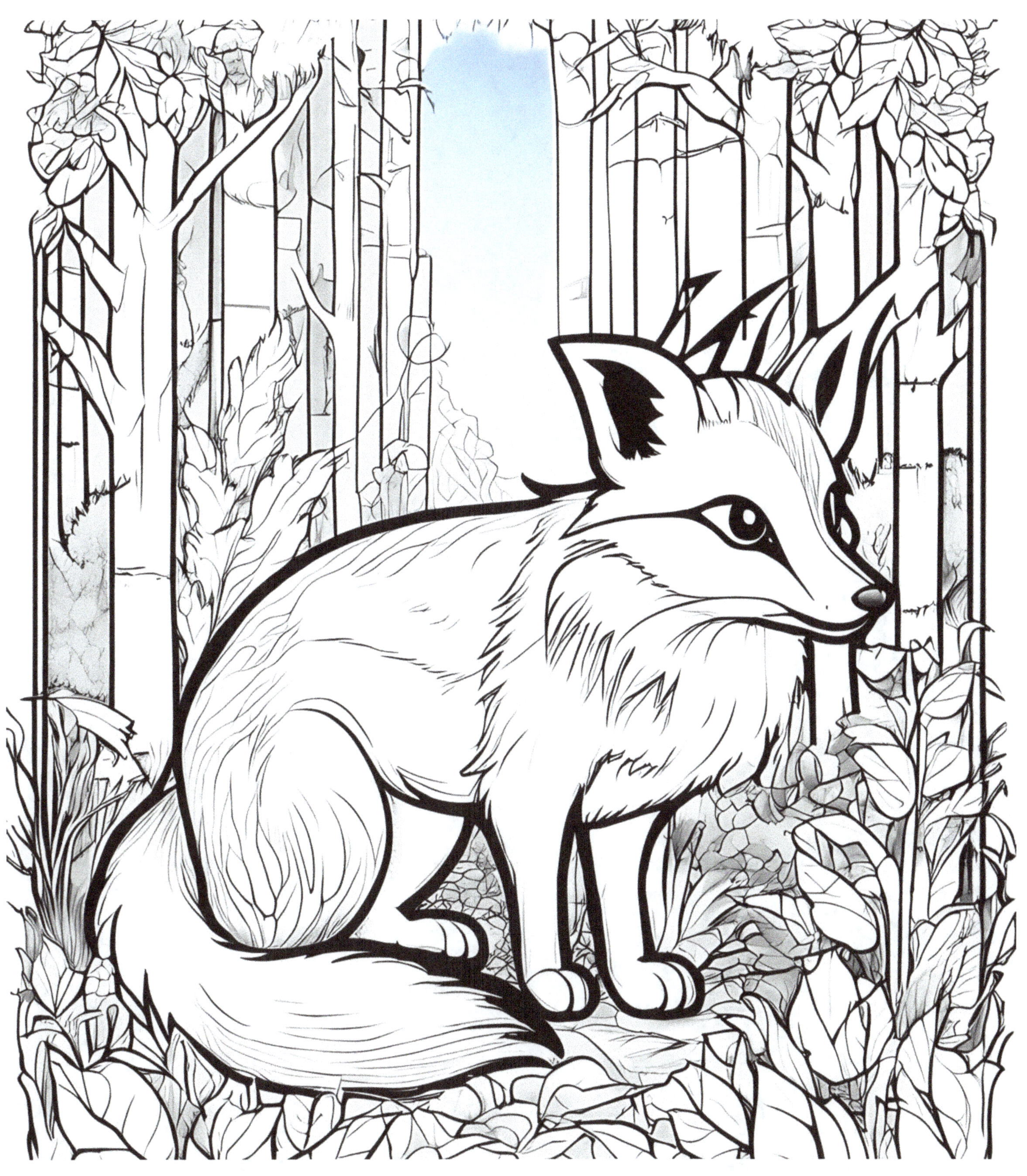

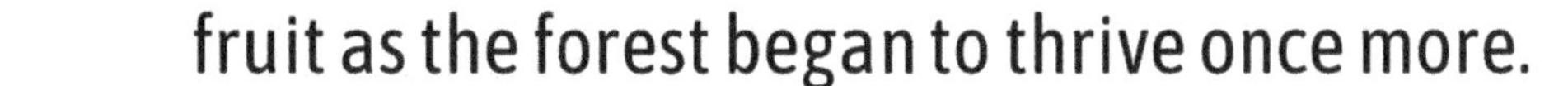

Determined to help, Lily rallied her friends together to save their beloved forest. They planted trees, cleaned up litter, and spread awareness about the importance of preserving nature. And with each passing day, their efforts bore fruit as the forest began to thrive once more.

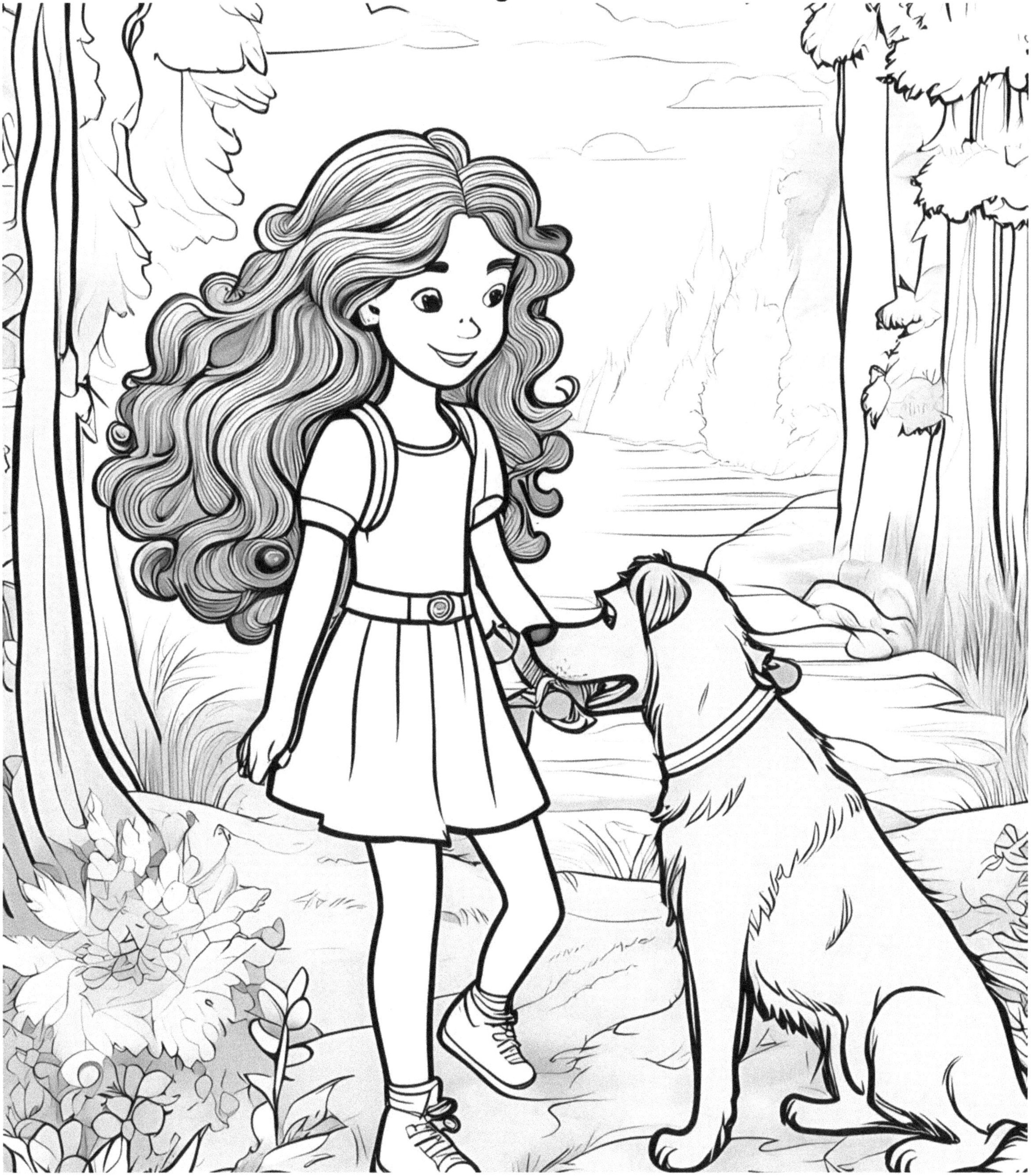

Through their adventures, Lily and her forest friends learned that friendship knows no bounds, and that by working together, they could overcome any obstacle. And as they gazed up at the starry sky each night, they knew that their bond would last forever.

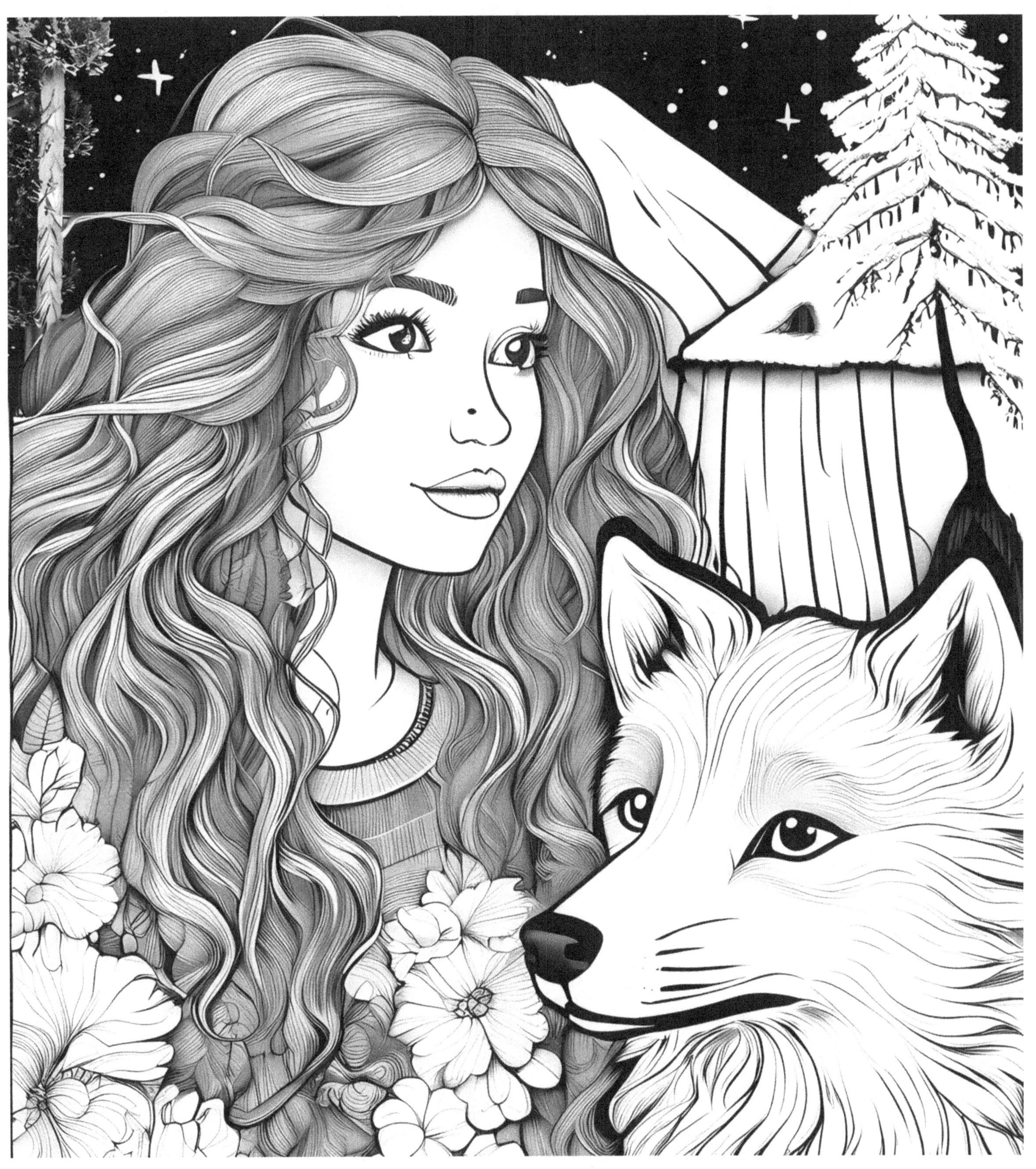

And so, the story of Lily, her dog and the Forest Friends comes to an end. But remember, the magic of friendship and the beauty of nature will always live on in our hearts.
Goodnight, and sweet dreams.

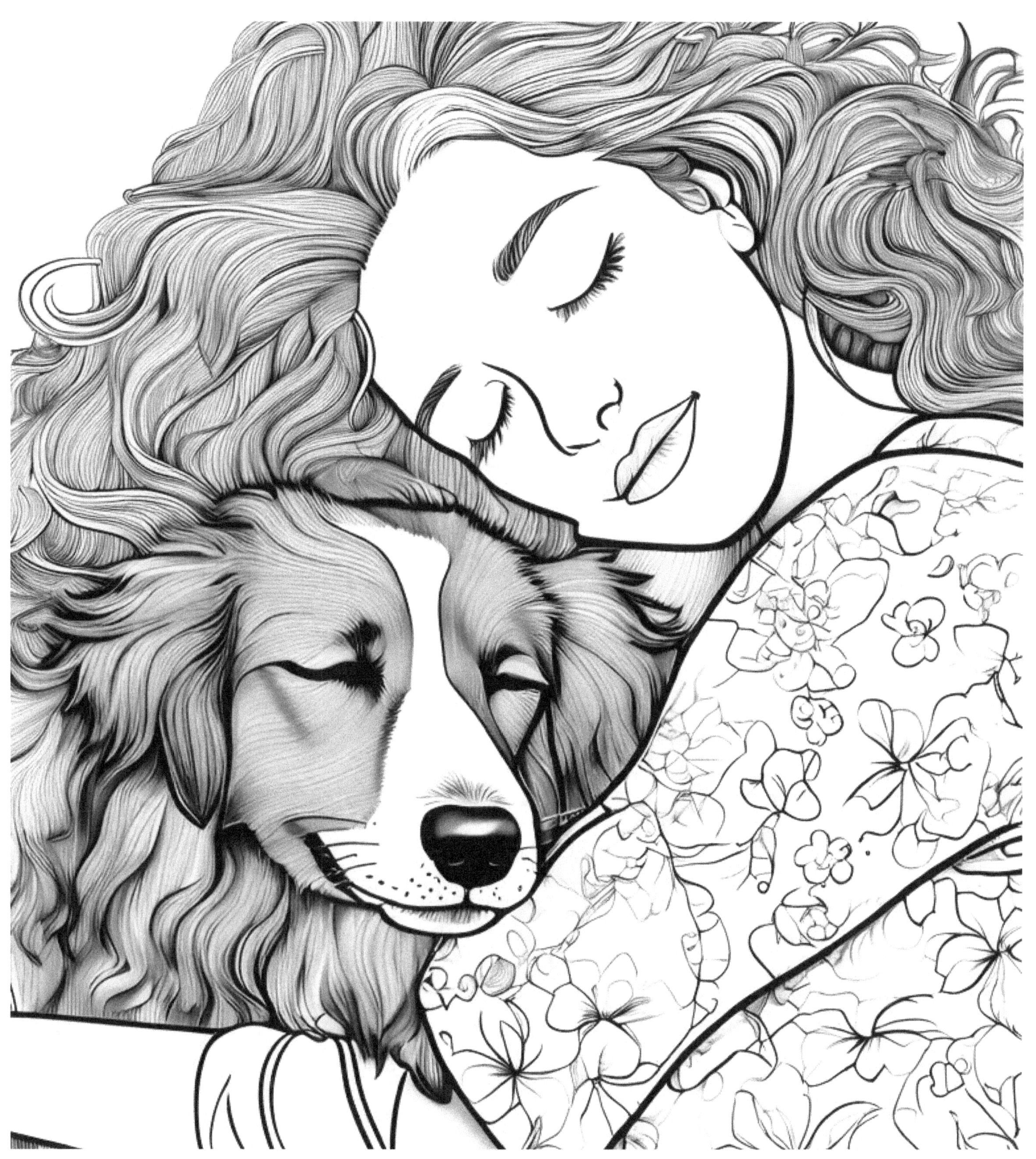

You're eager for more painting!
Here are some more examples!

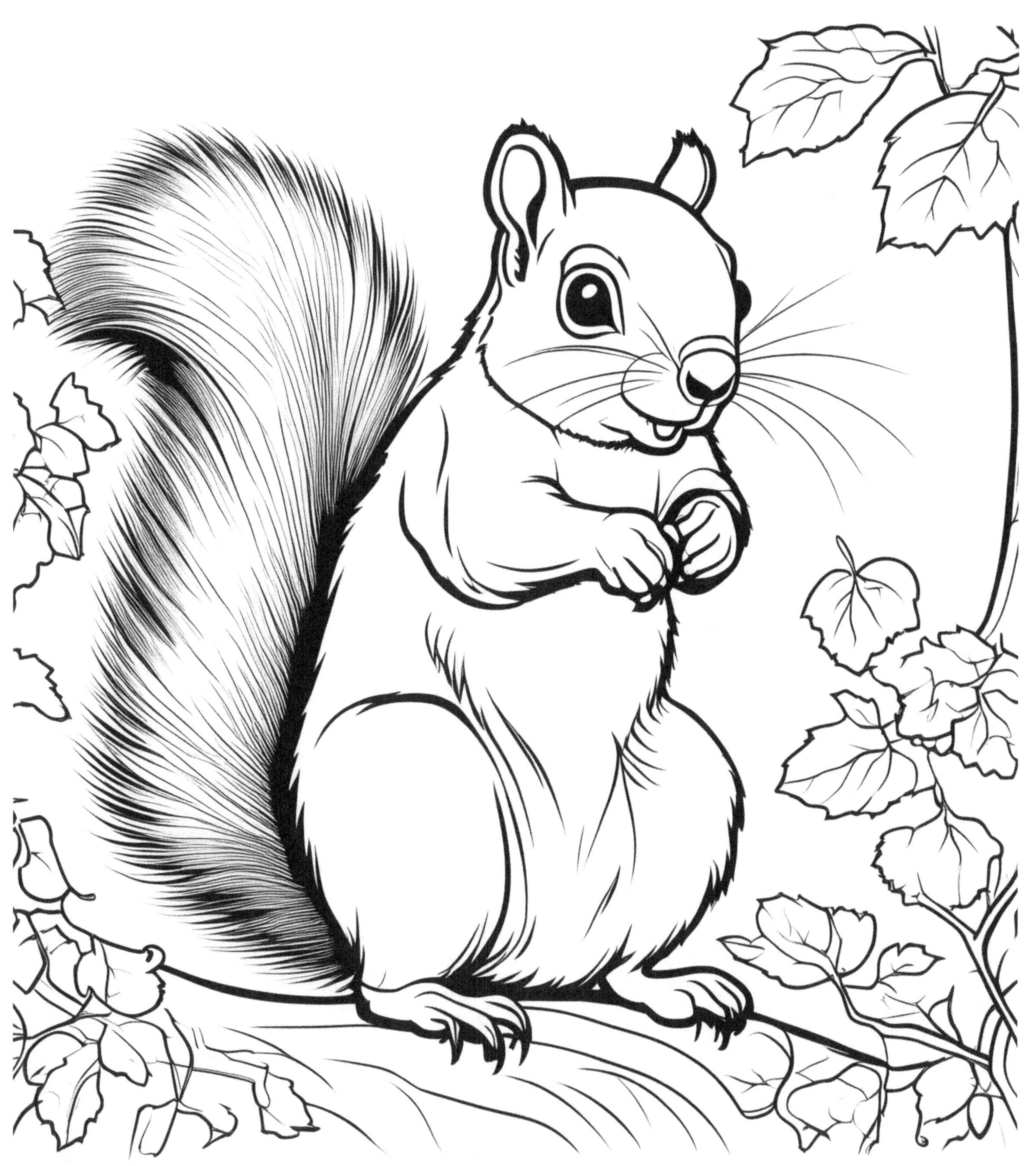

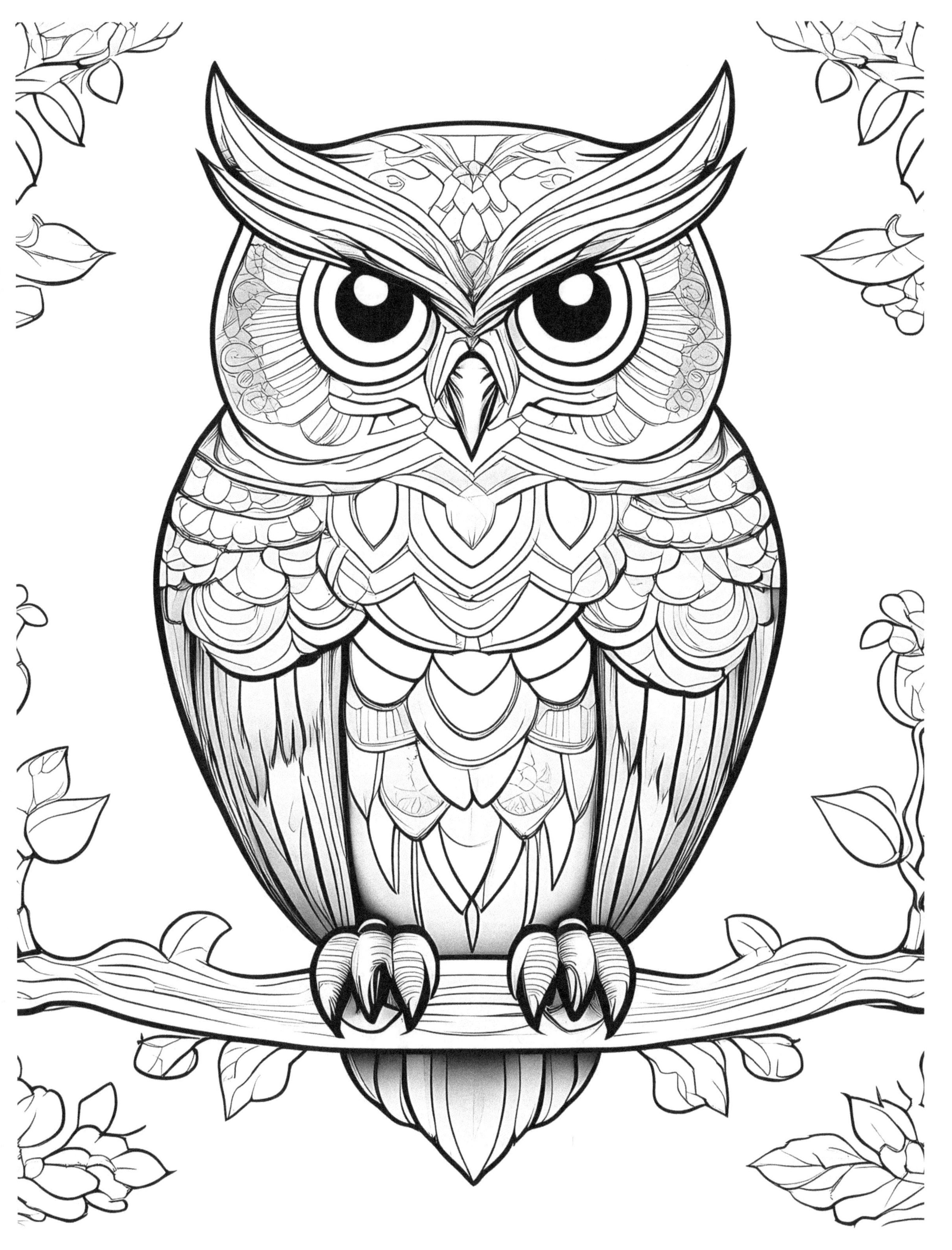

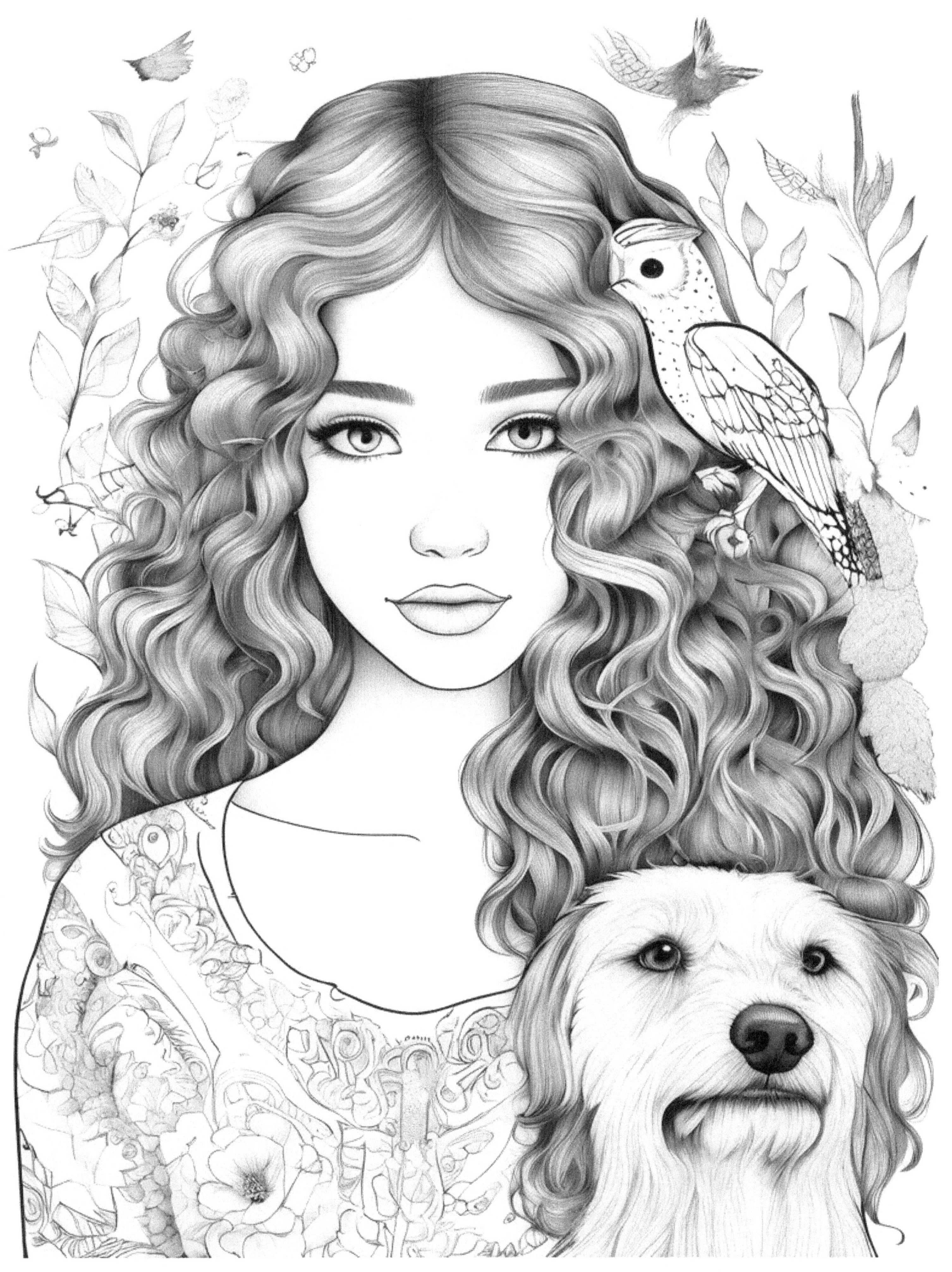

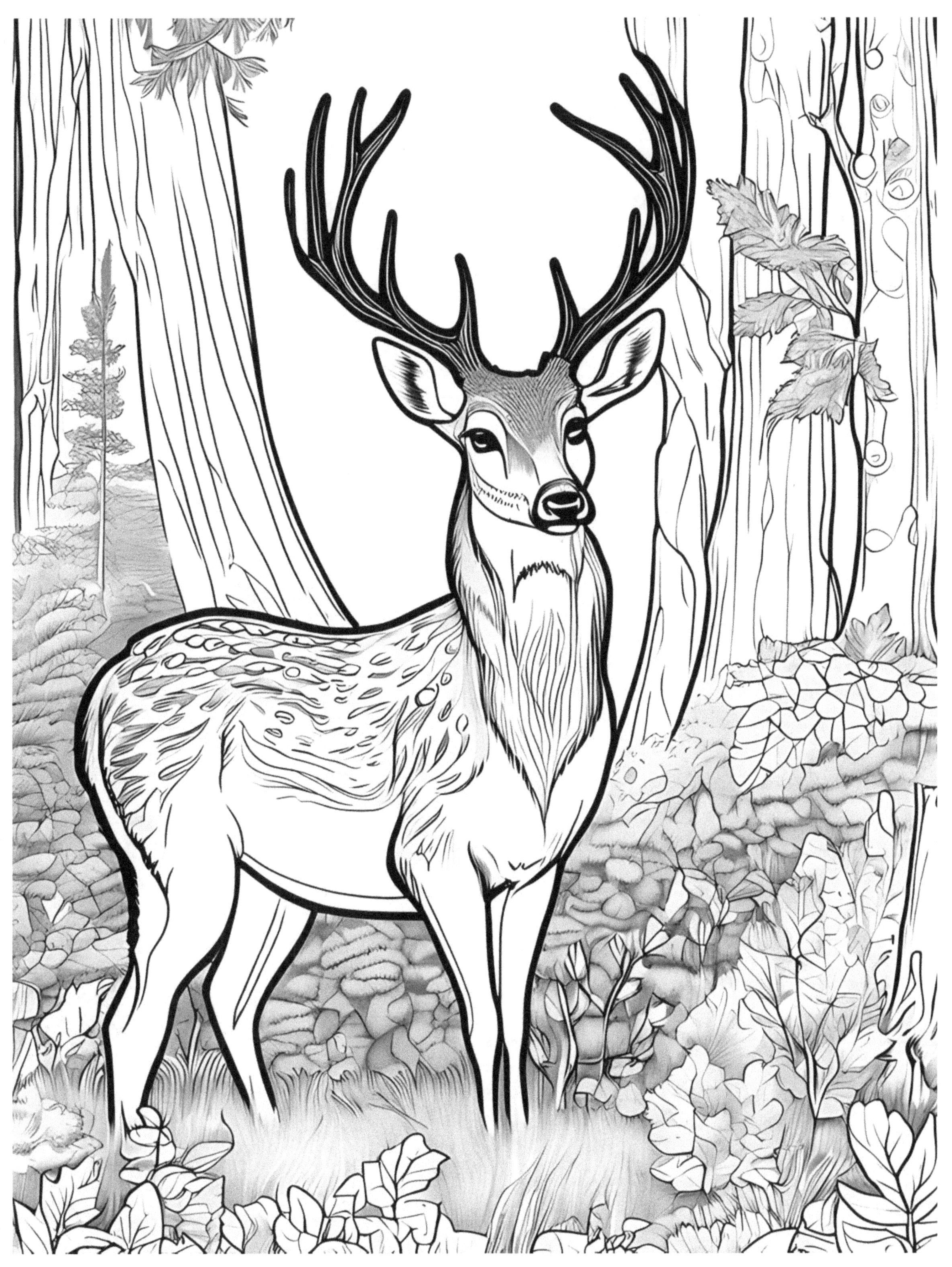

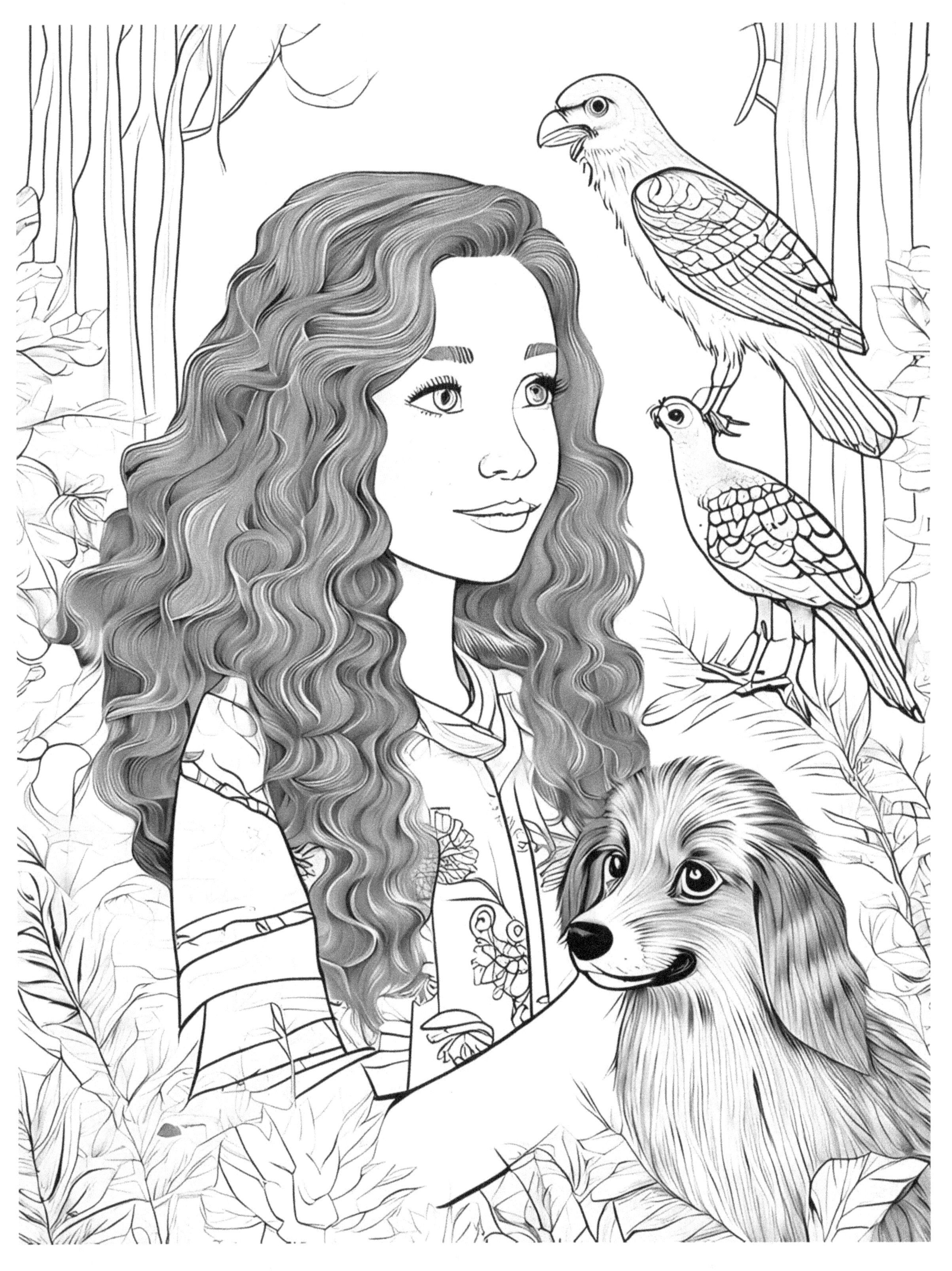

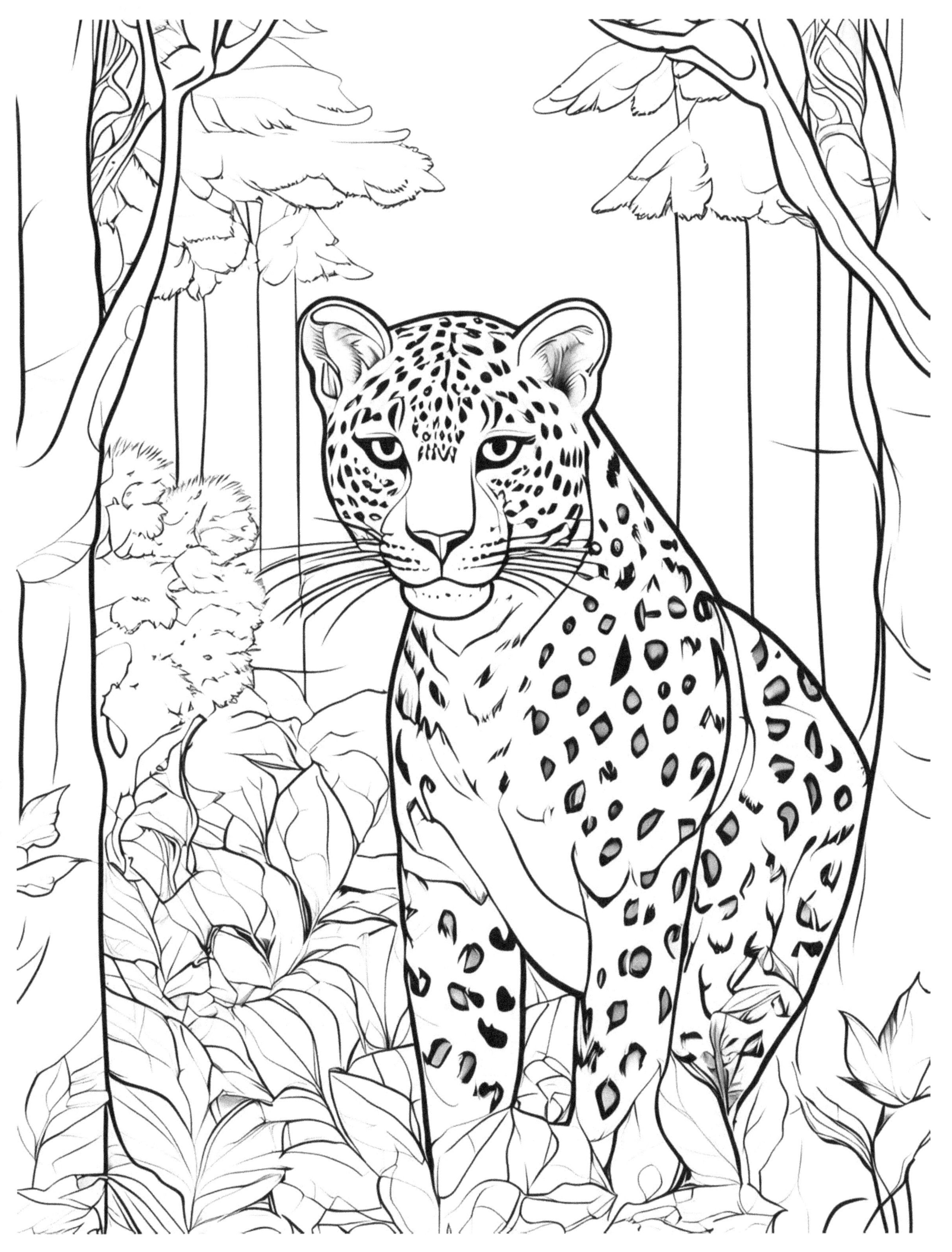

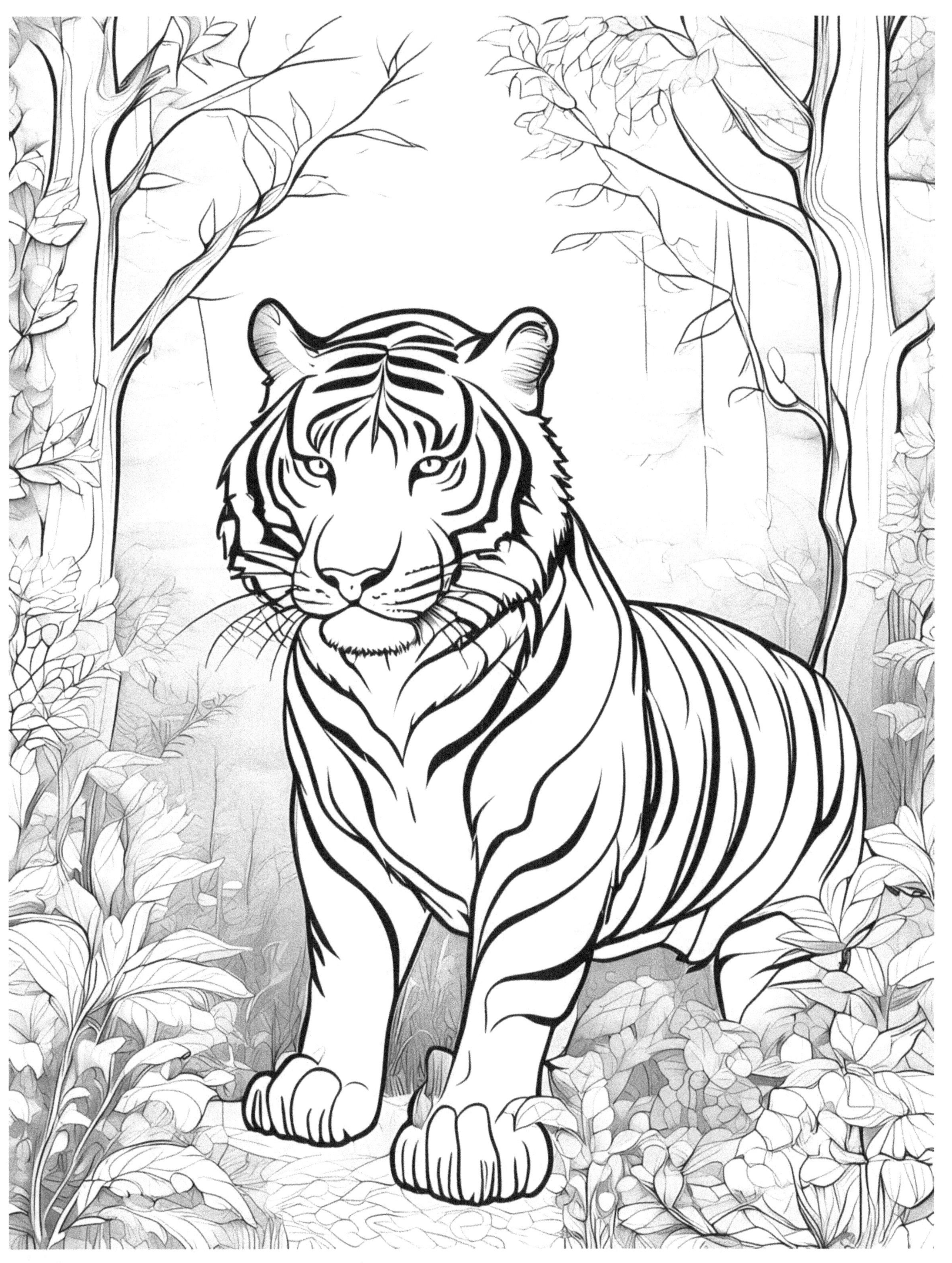

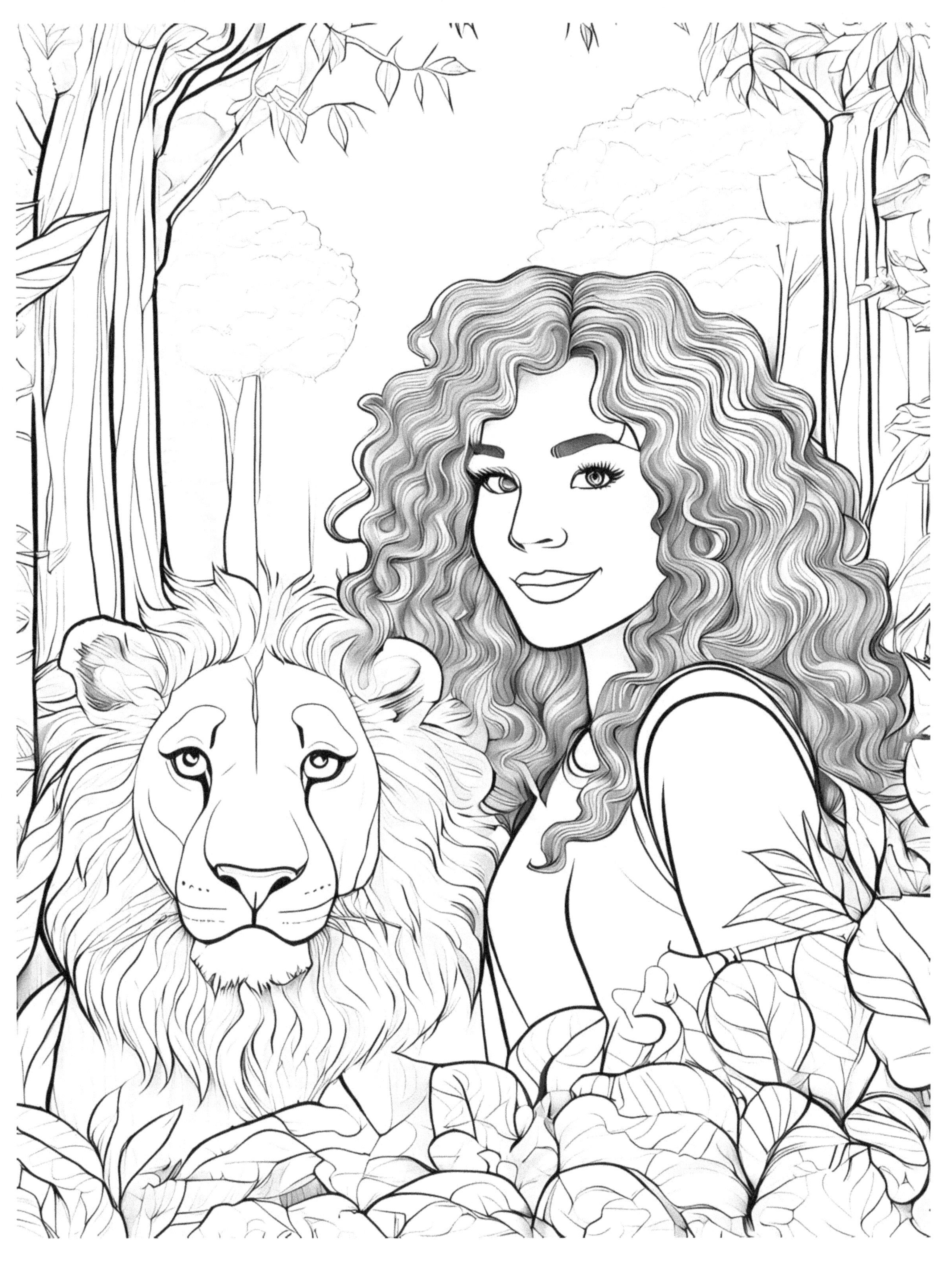

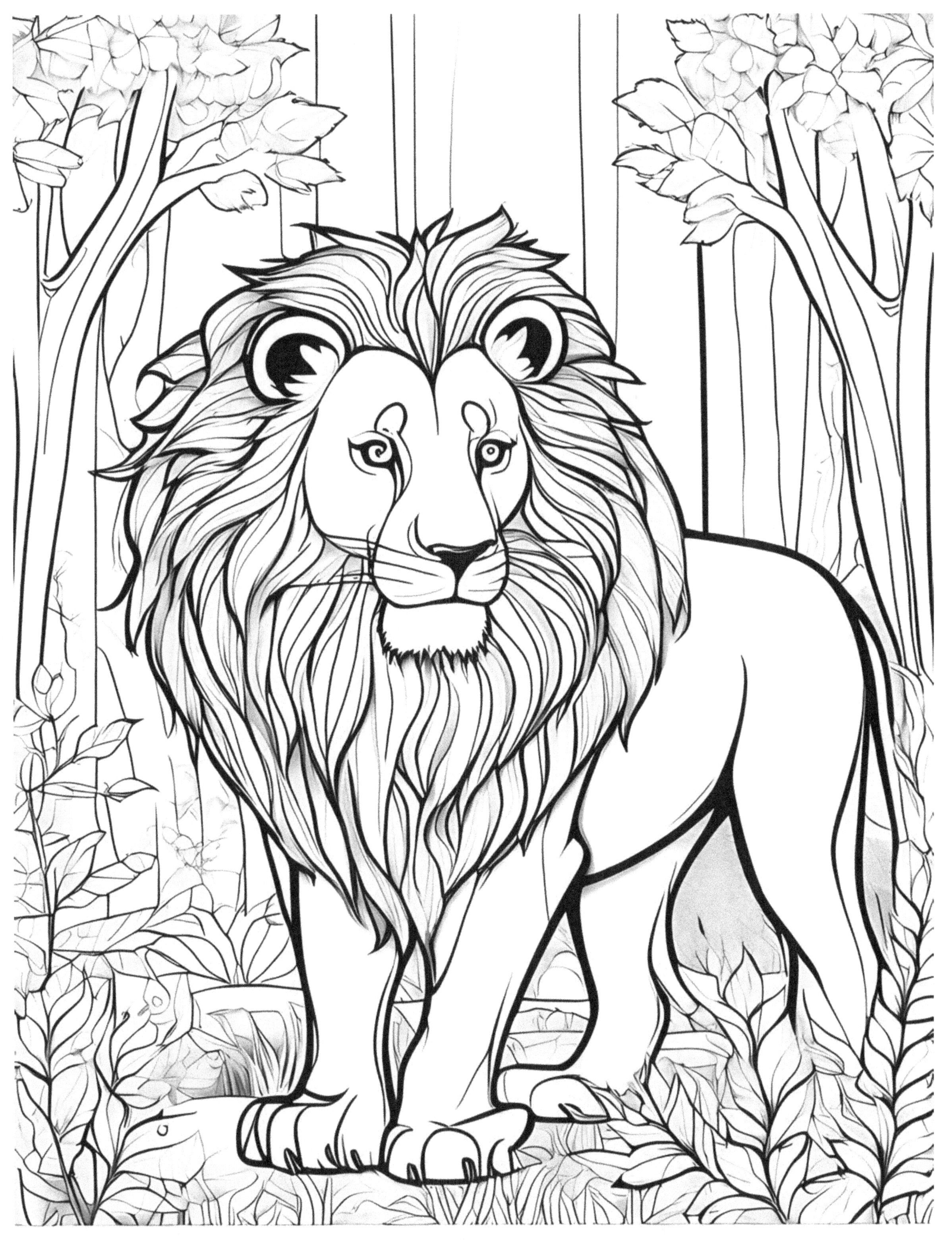

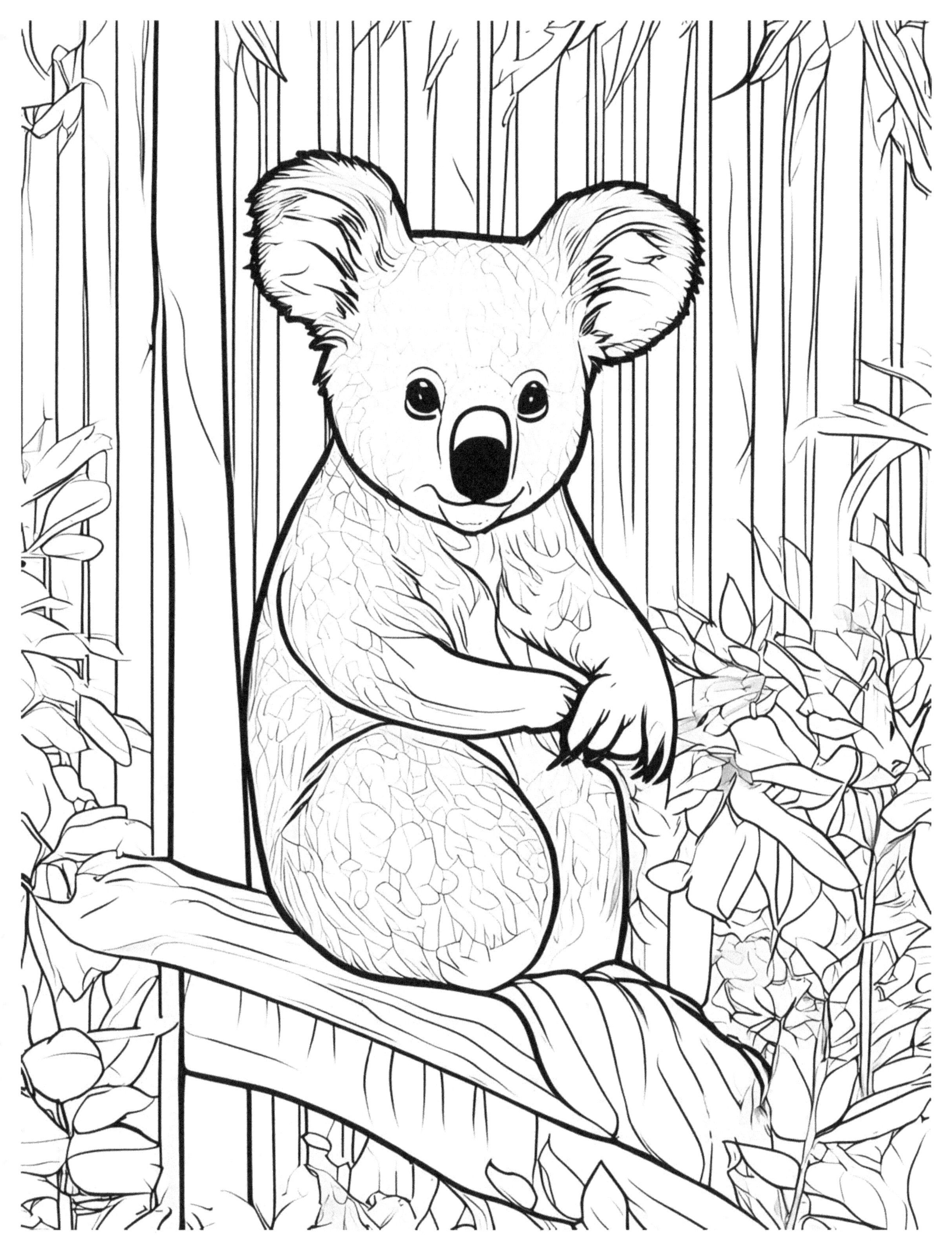

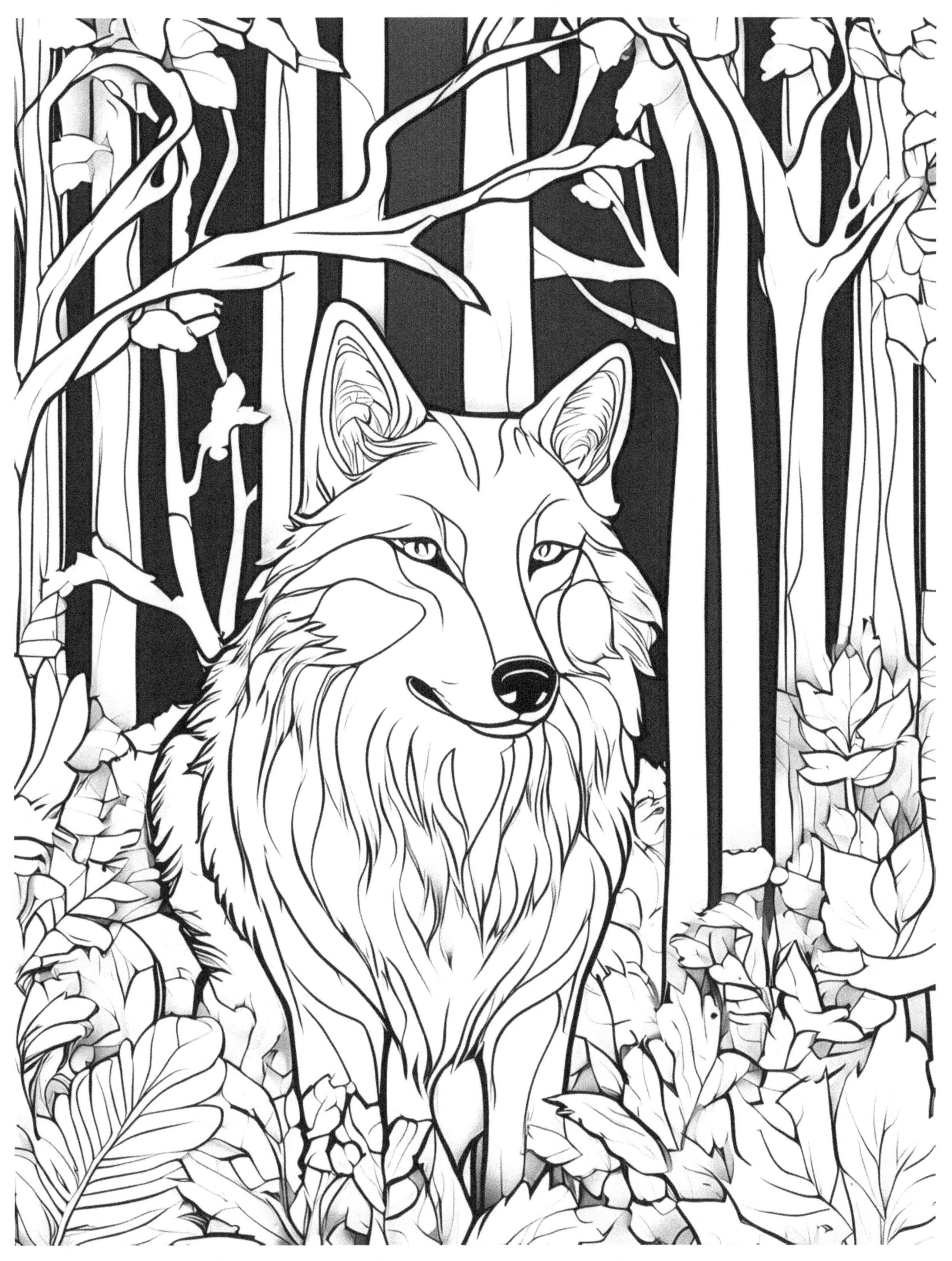

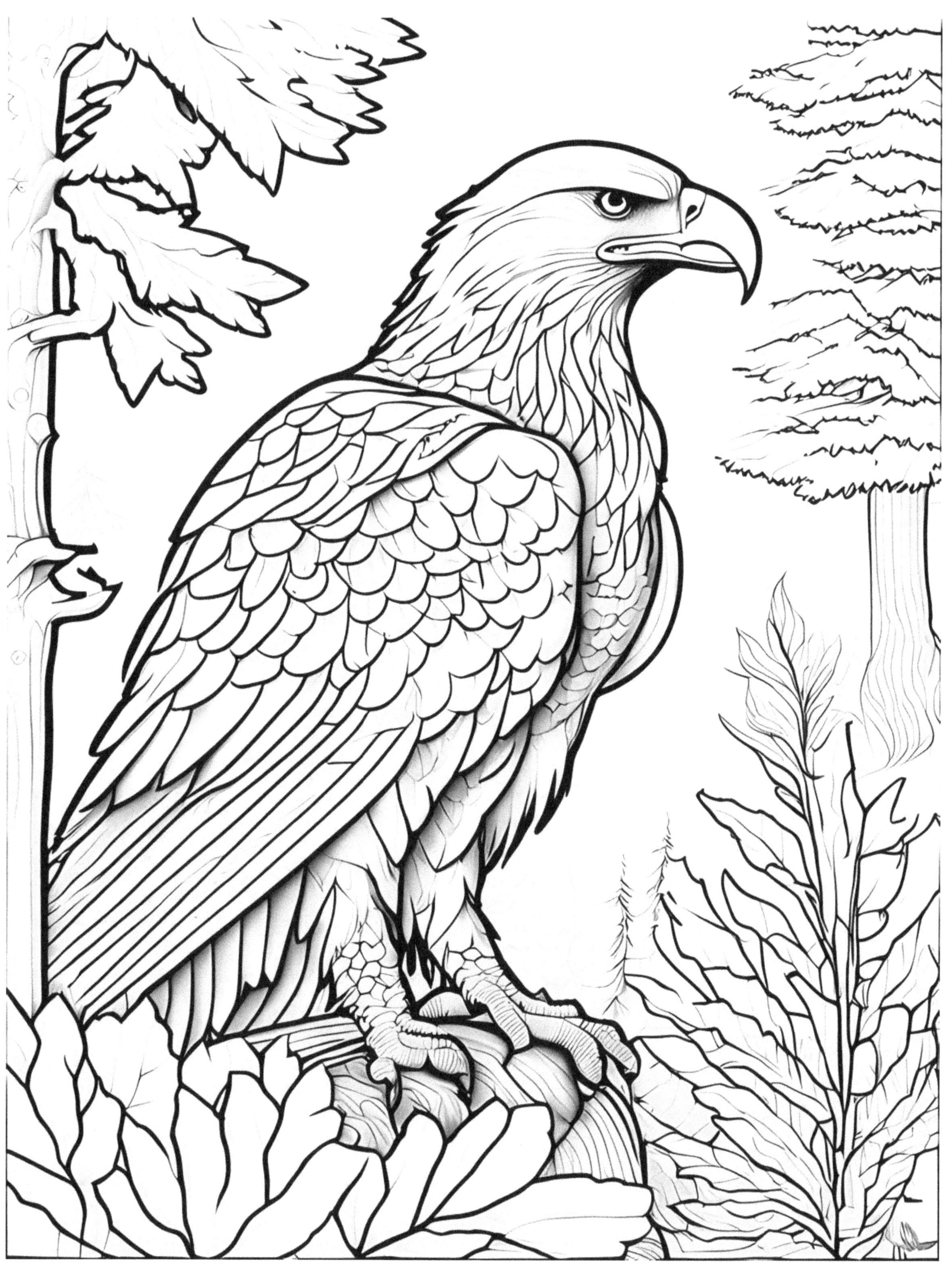

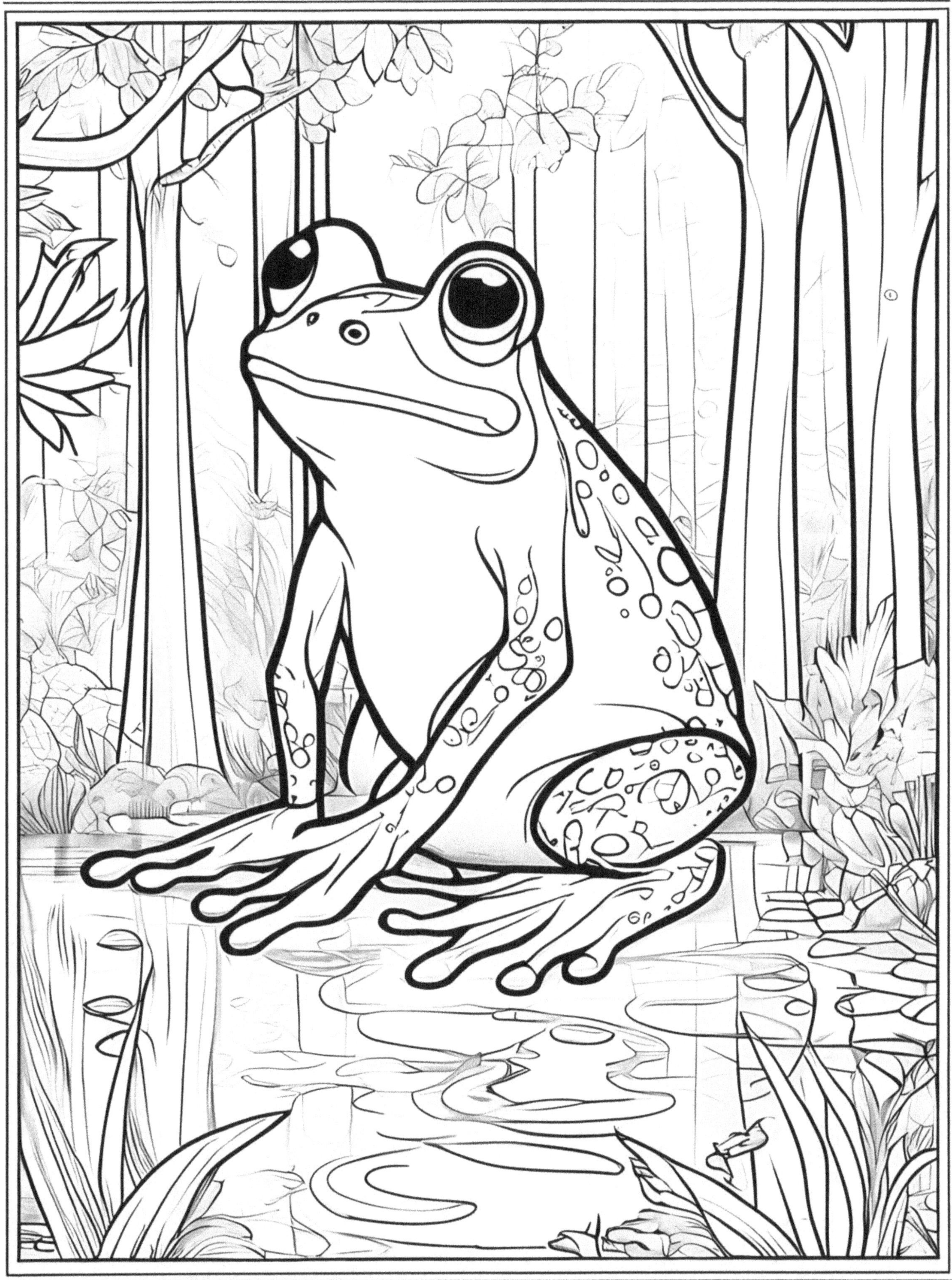

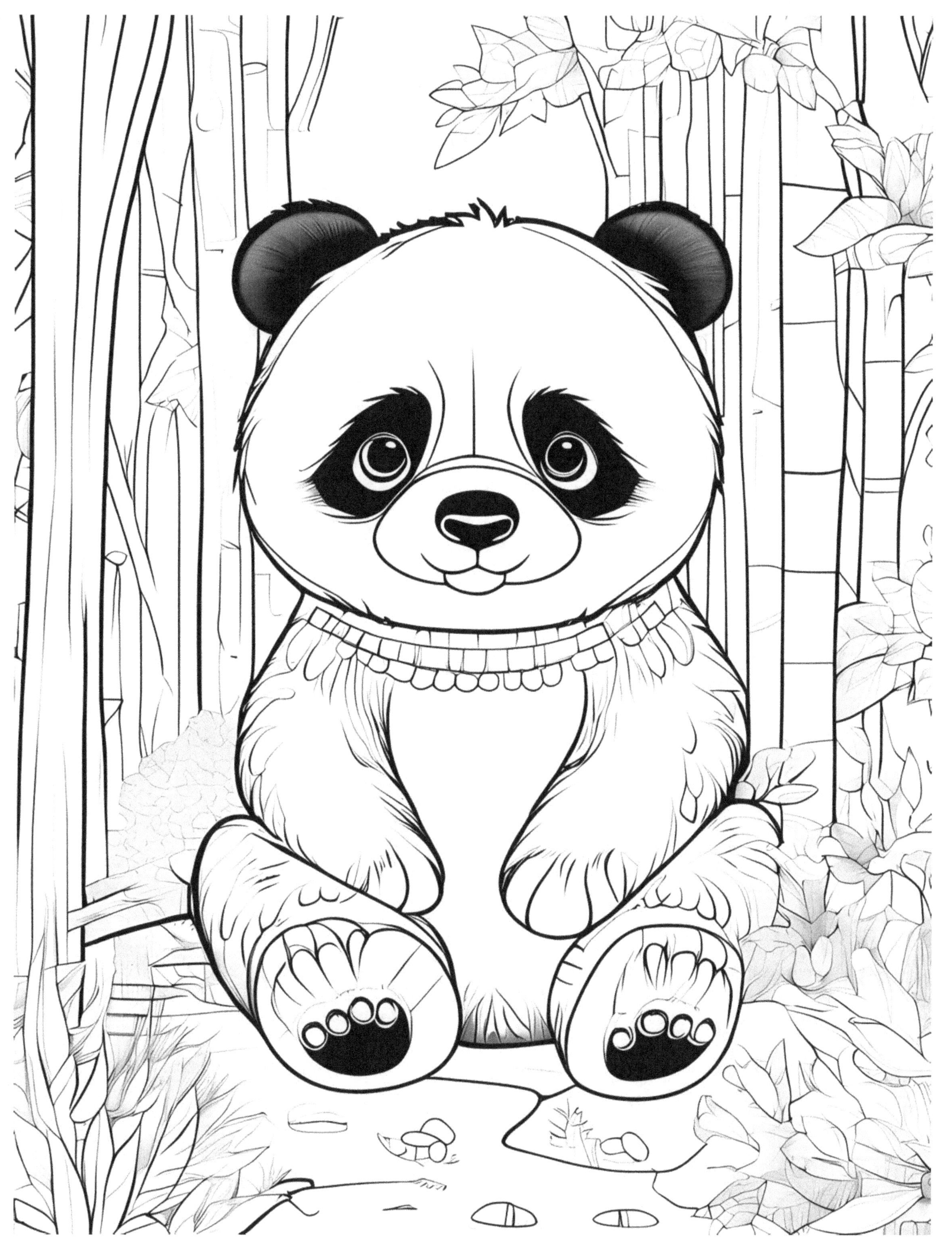

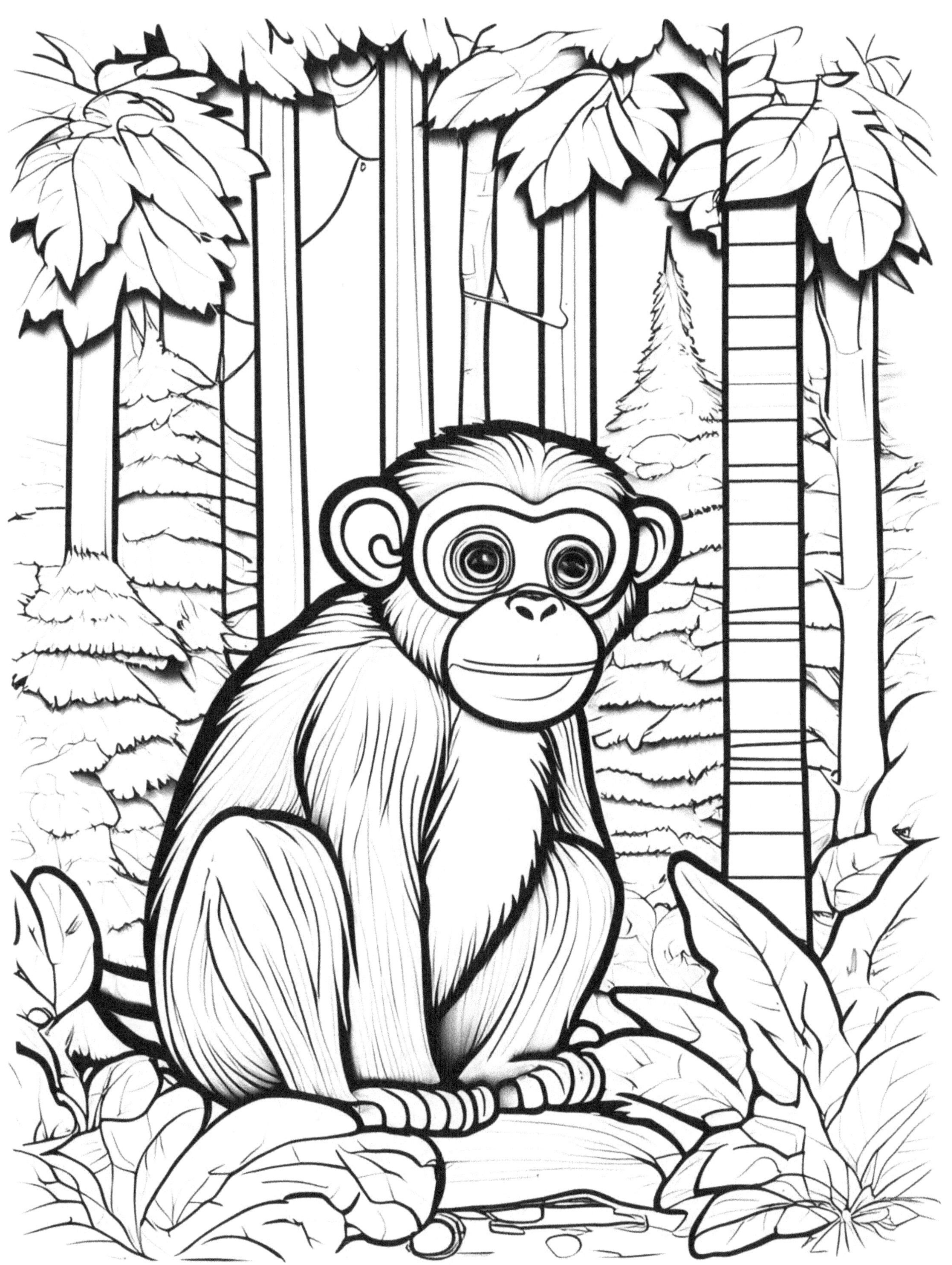

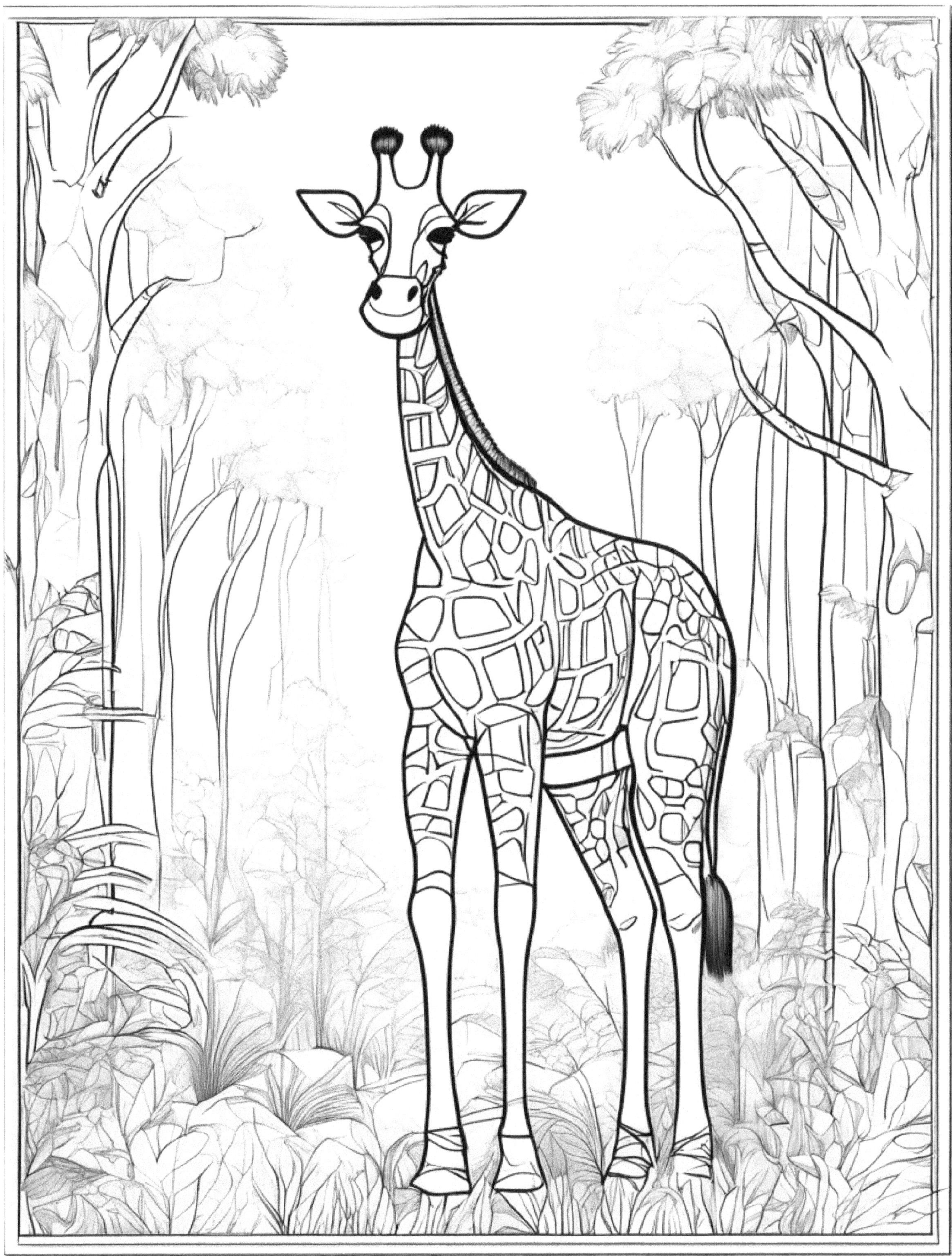

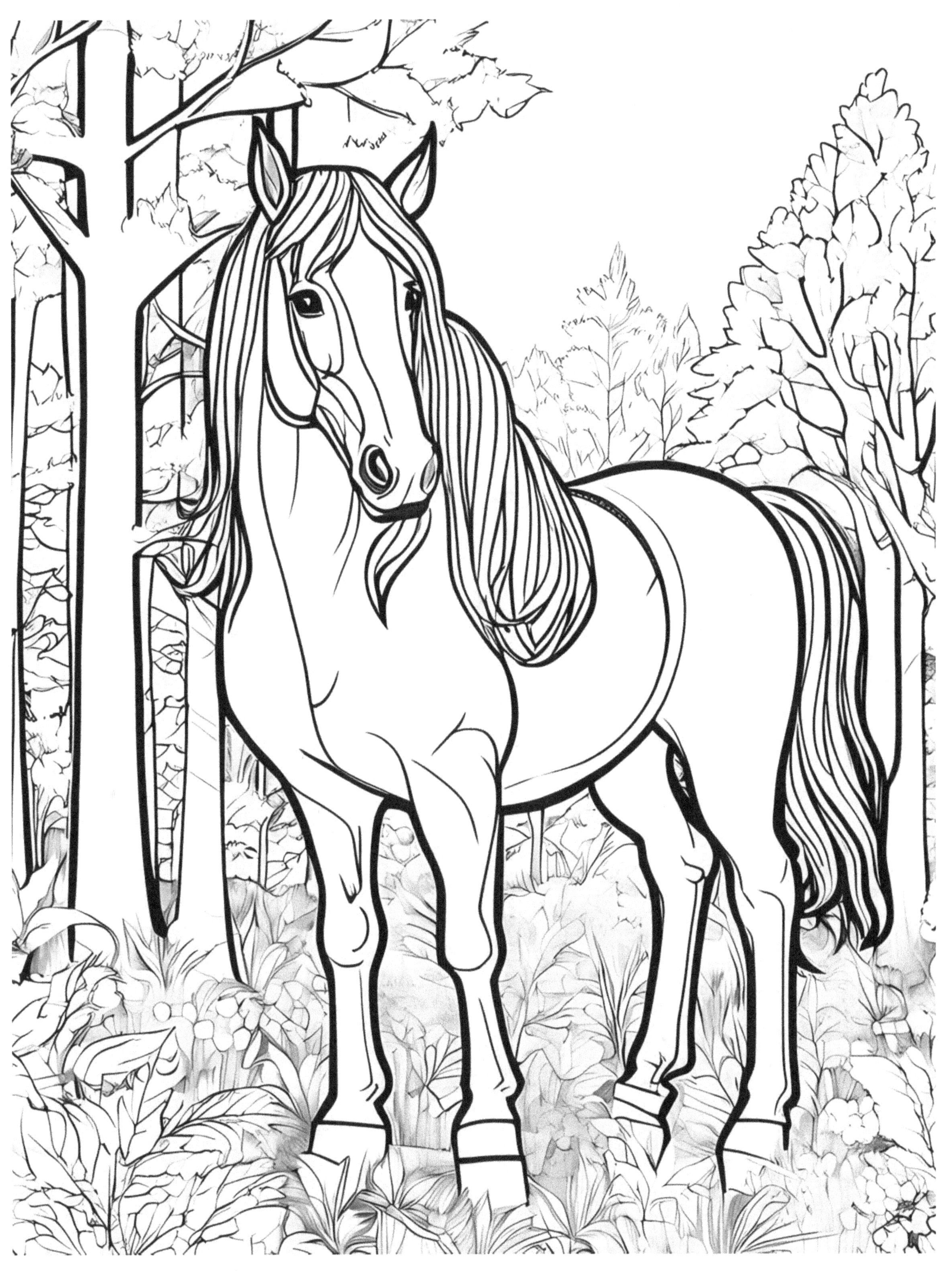

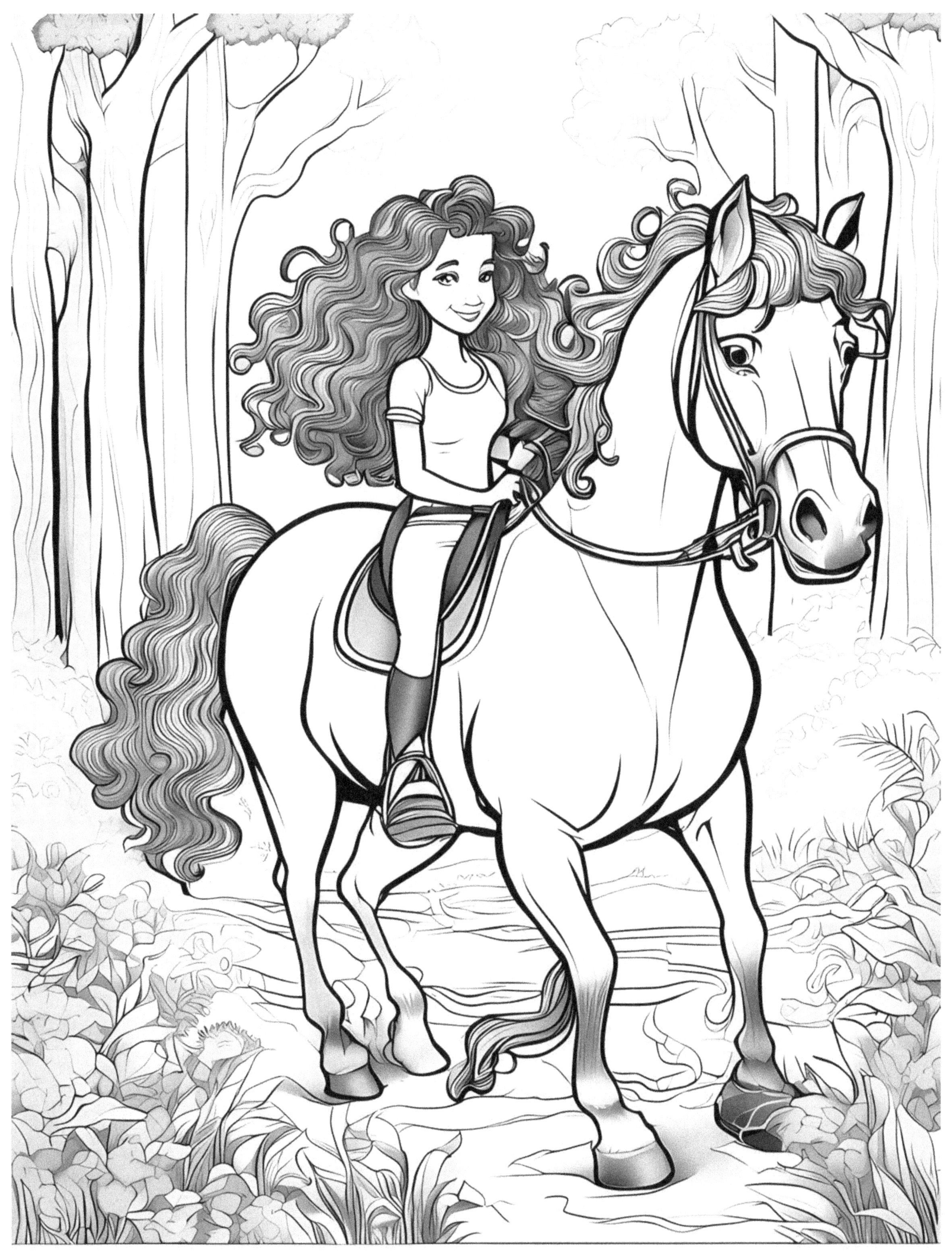

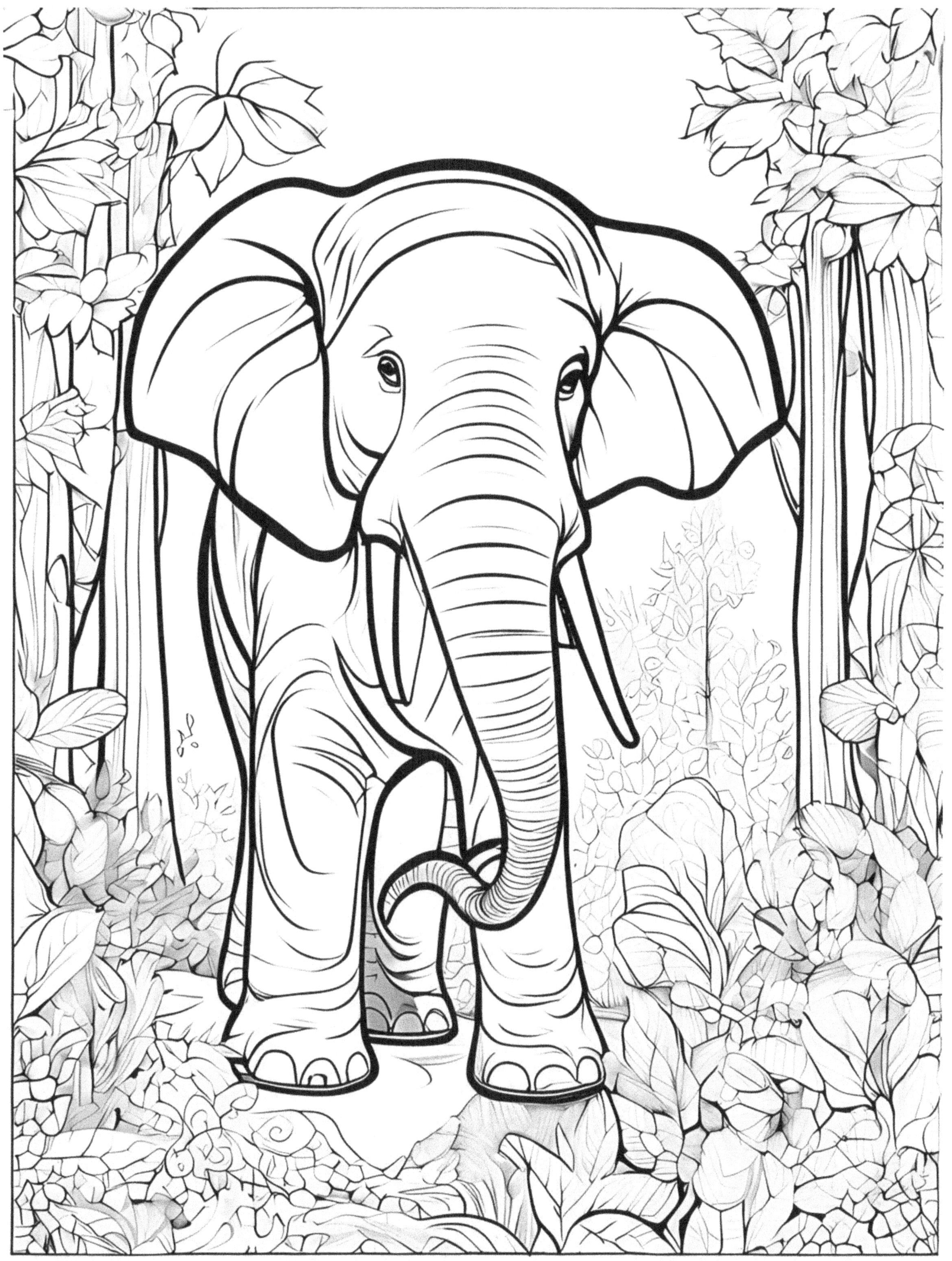

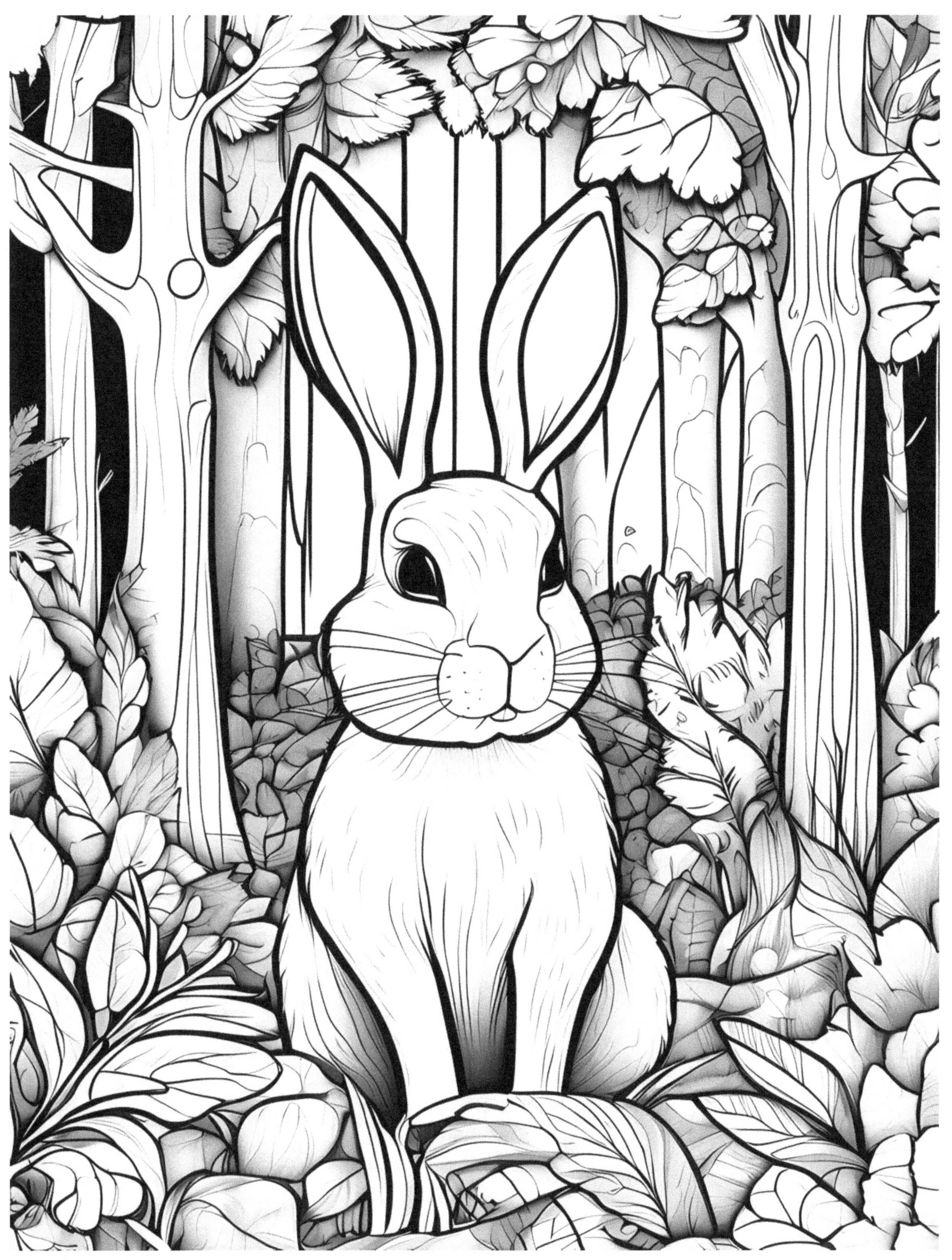

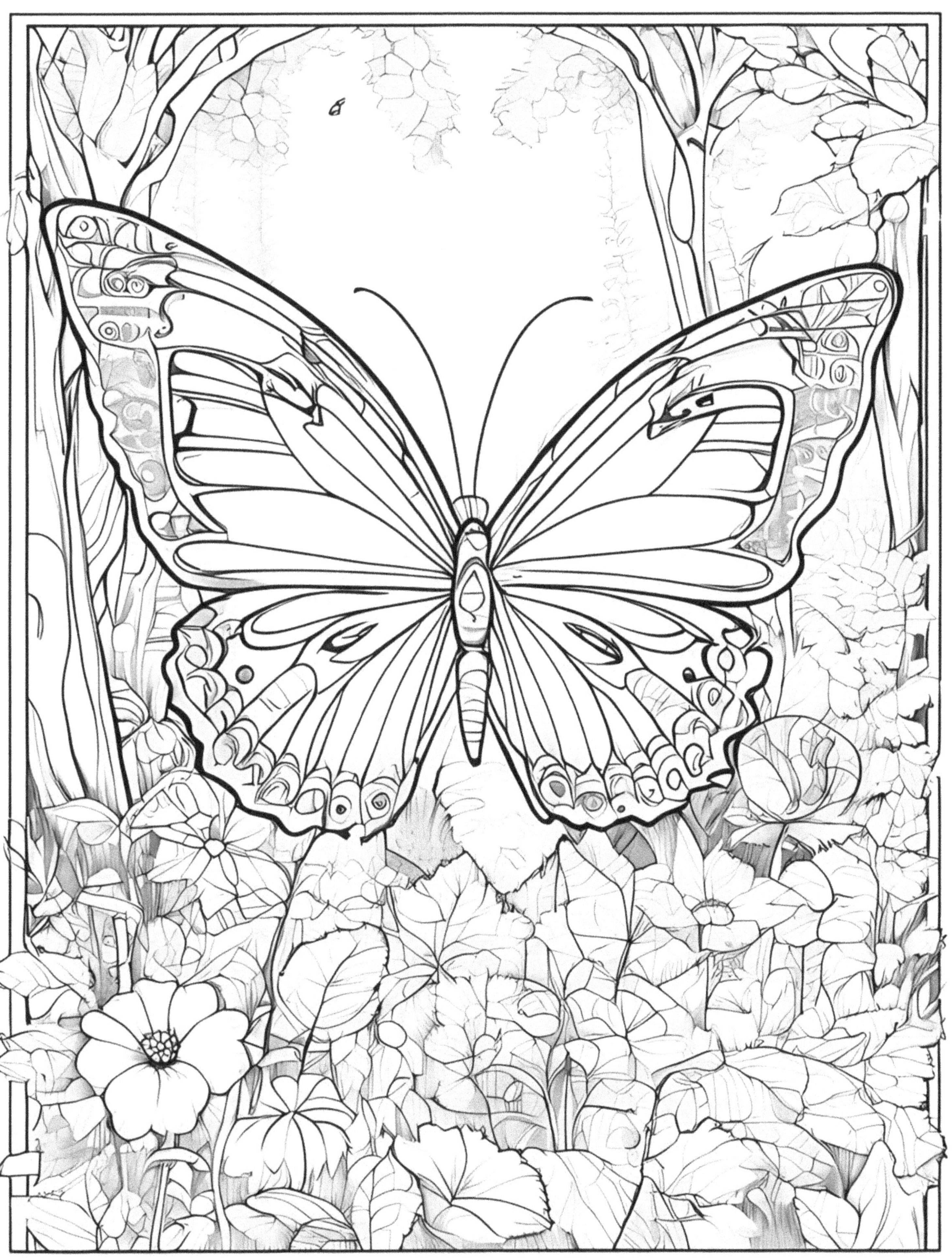

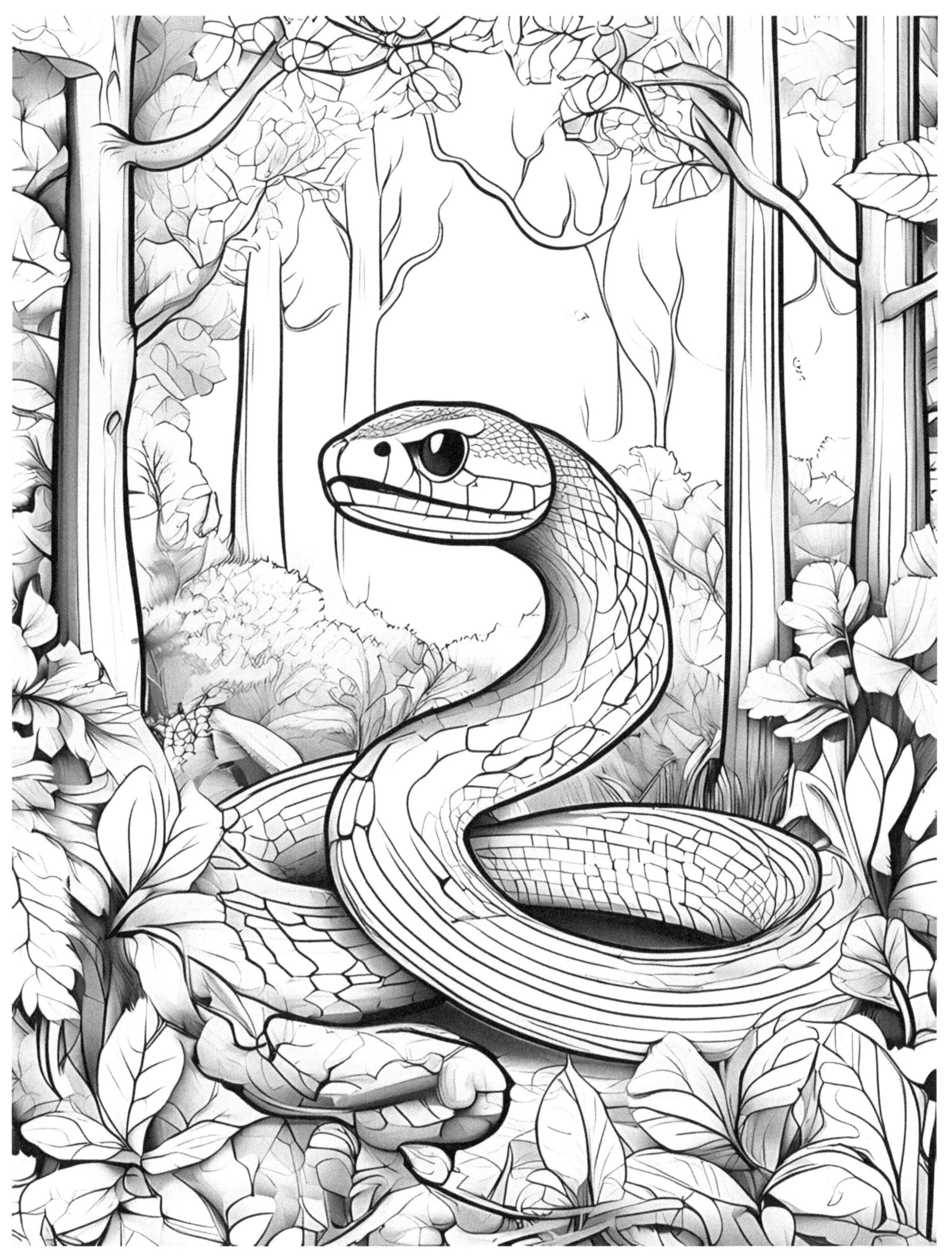

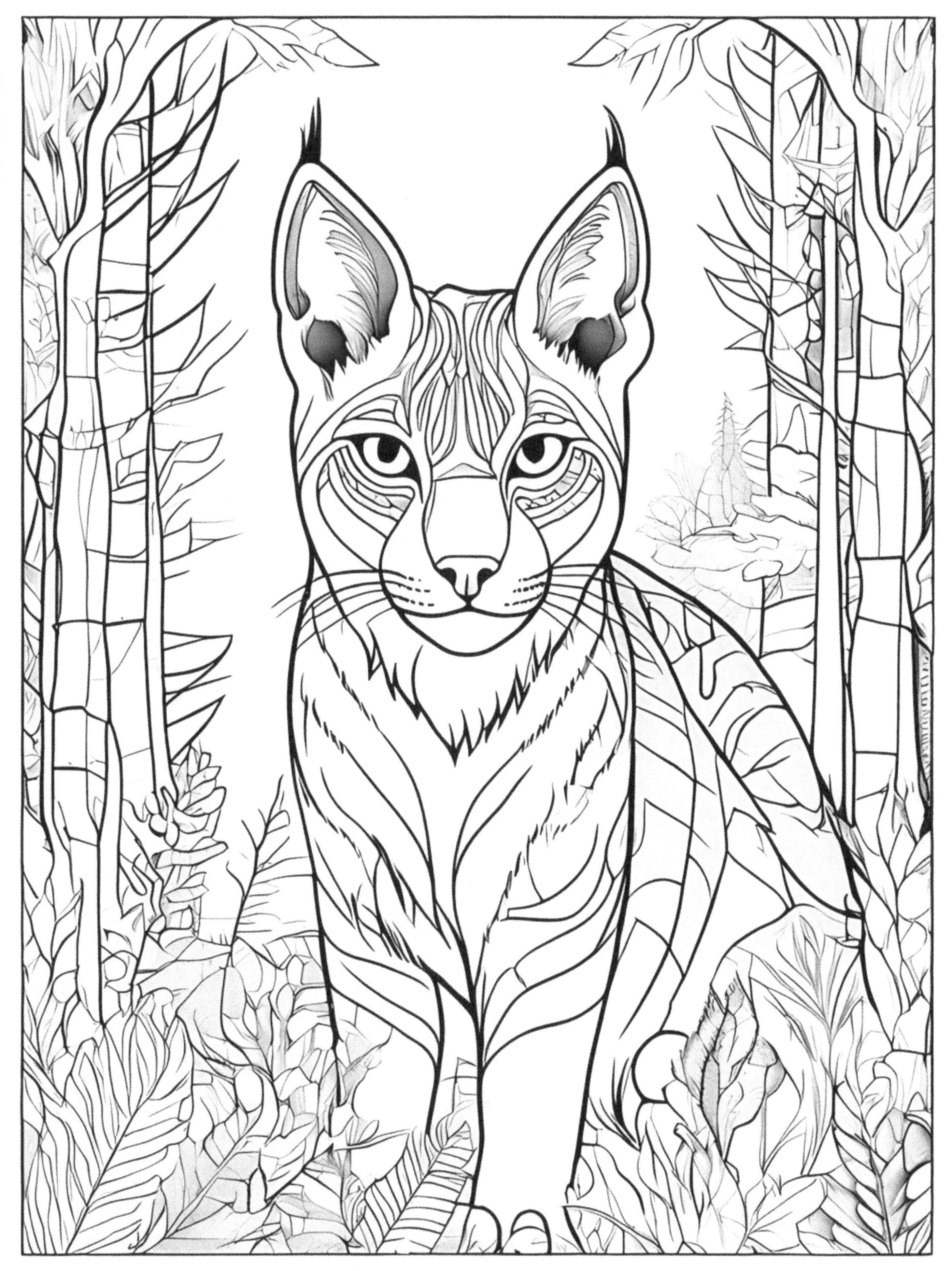

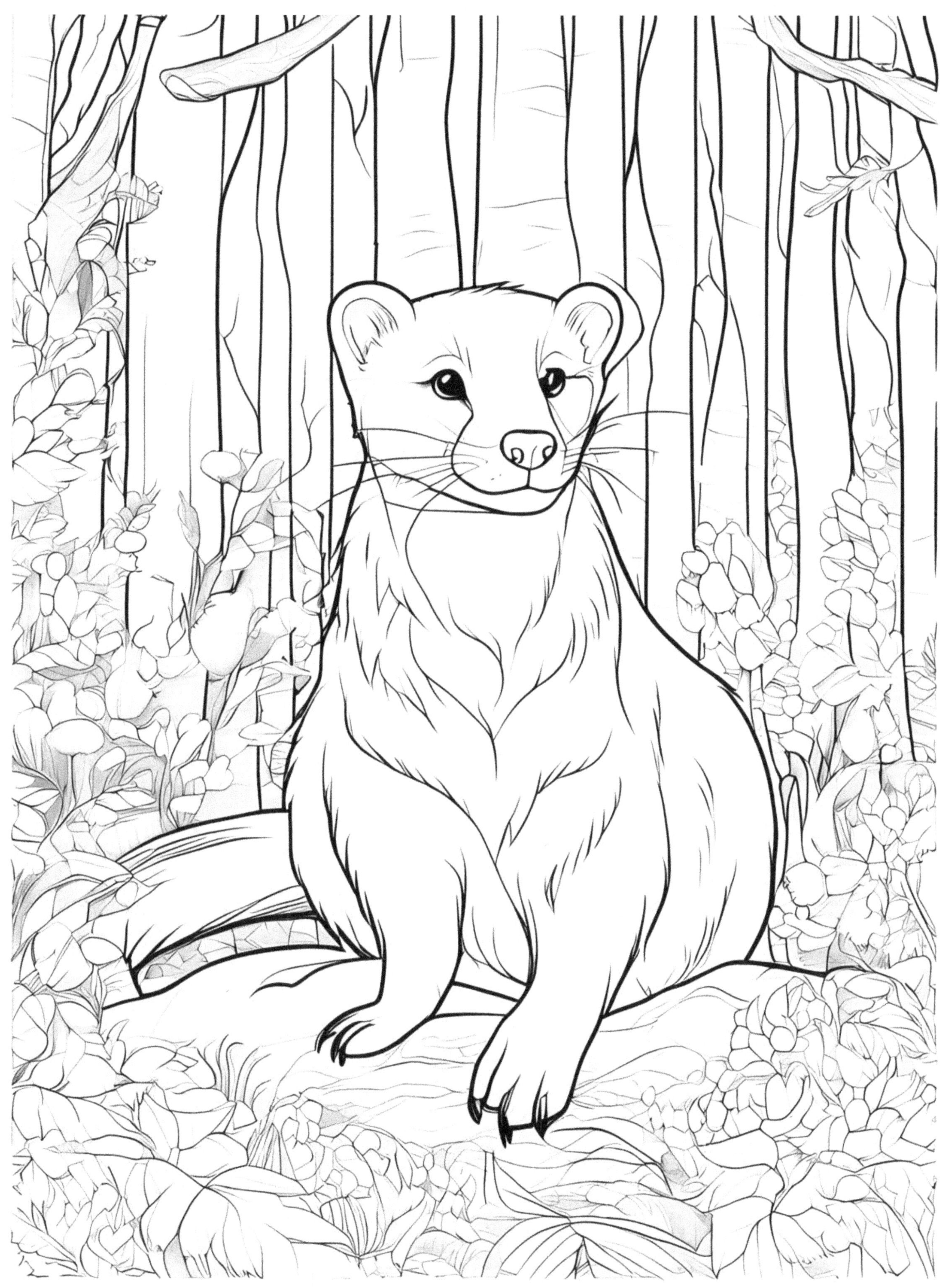

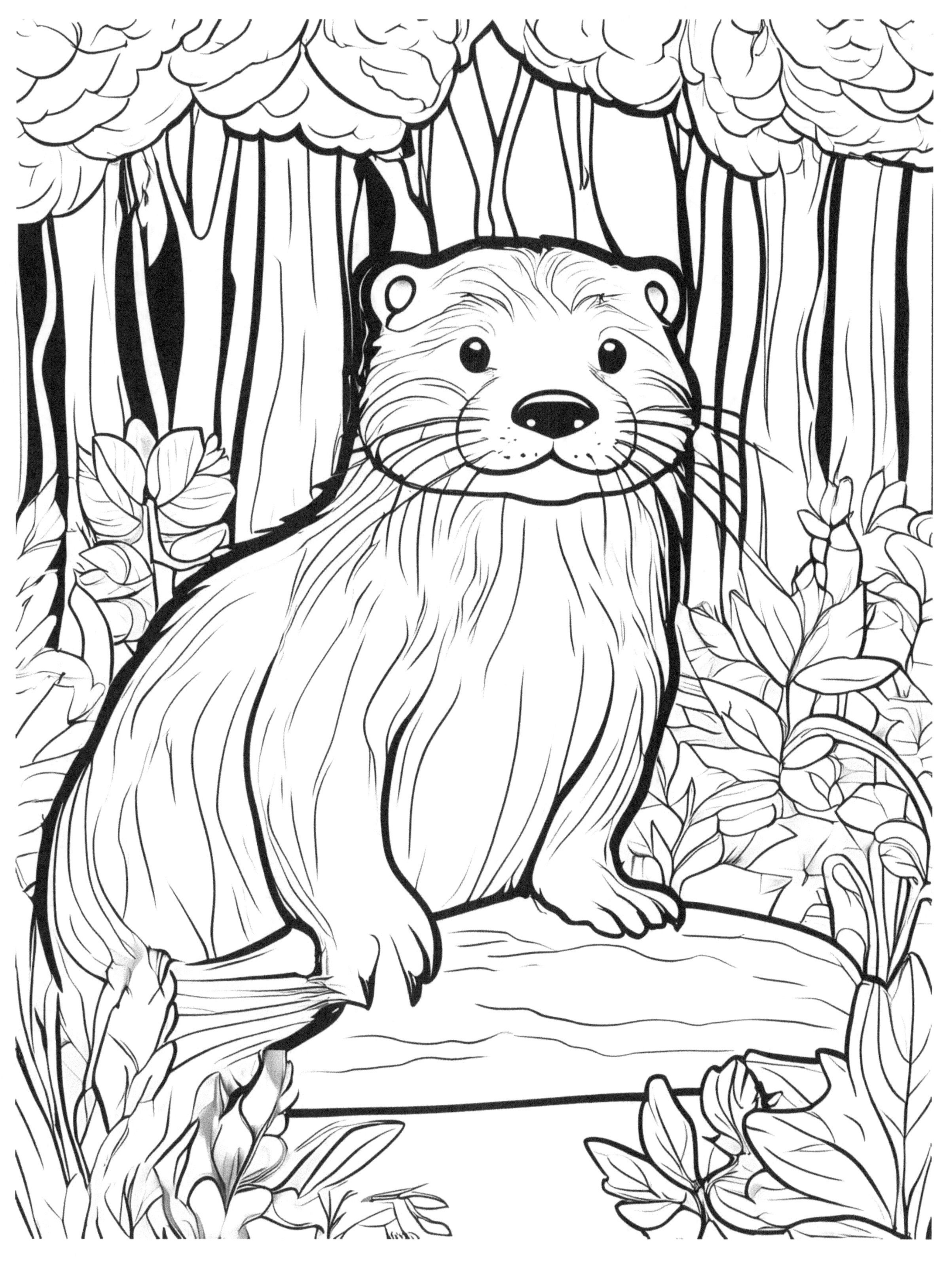

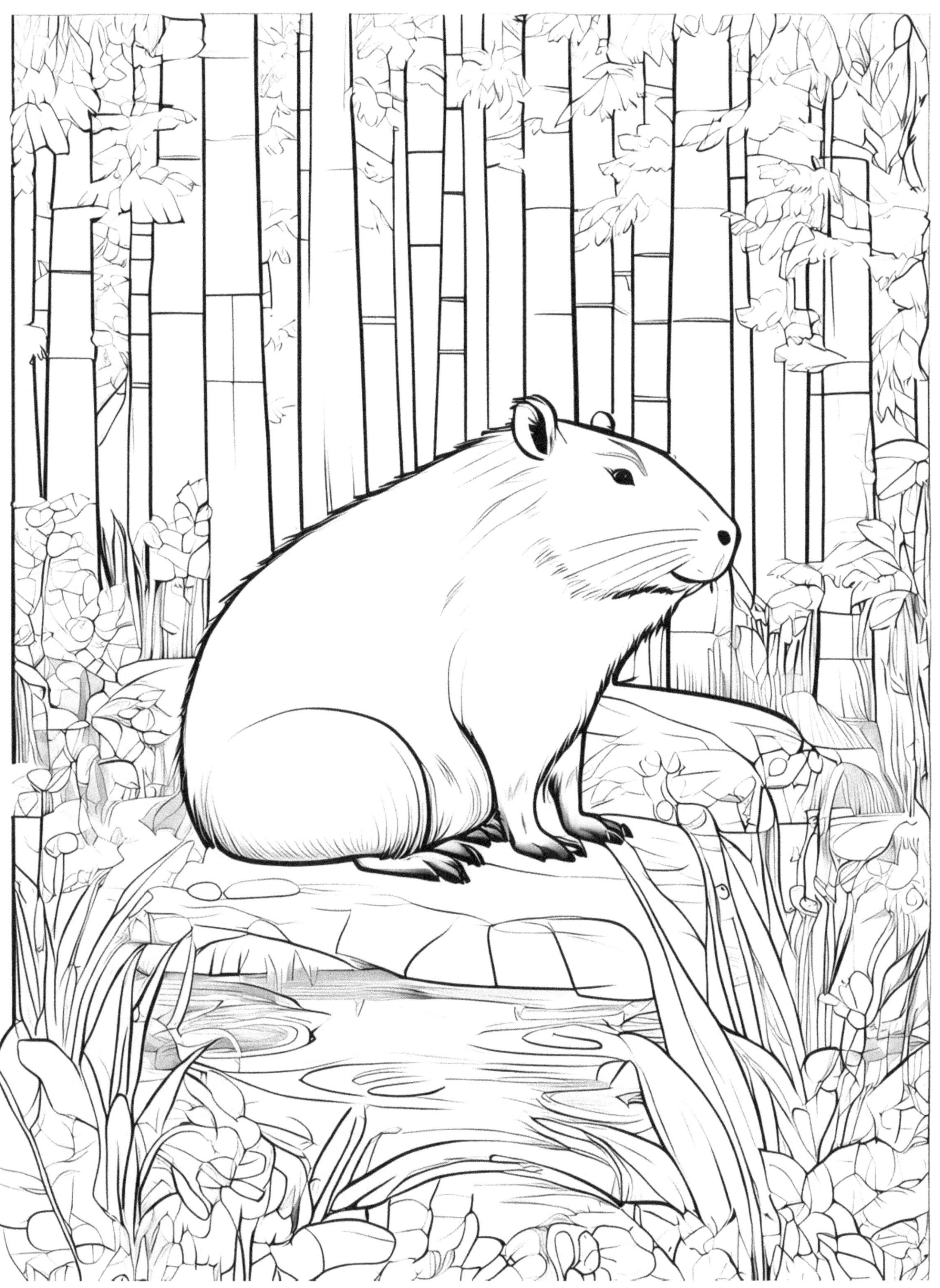

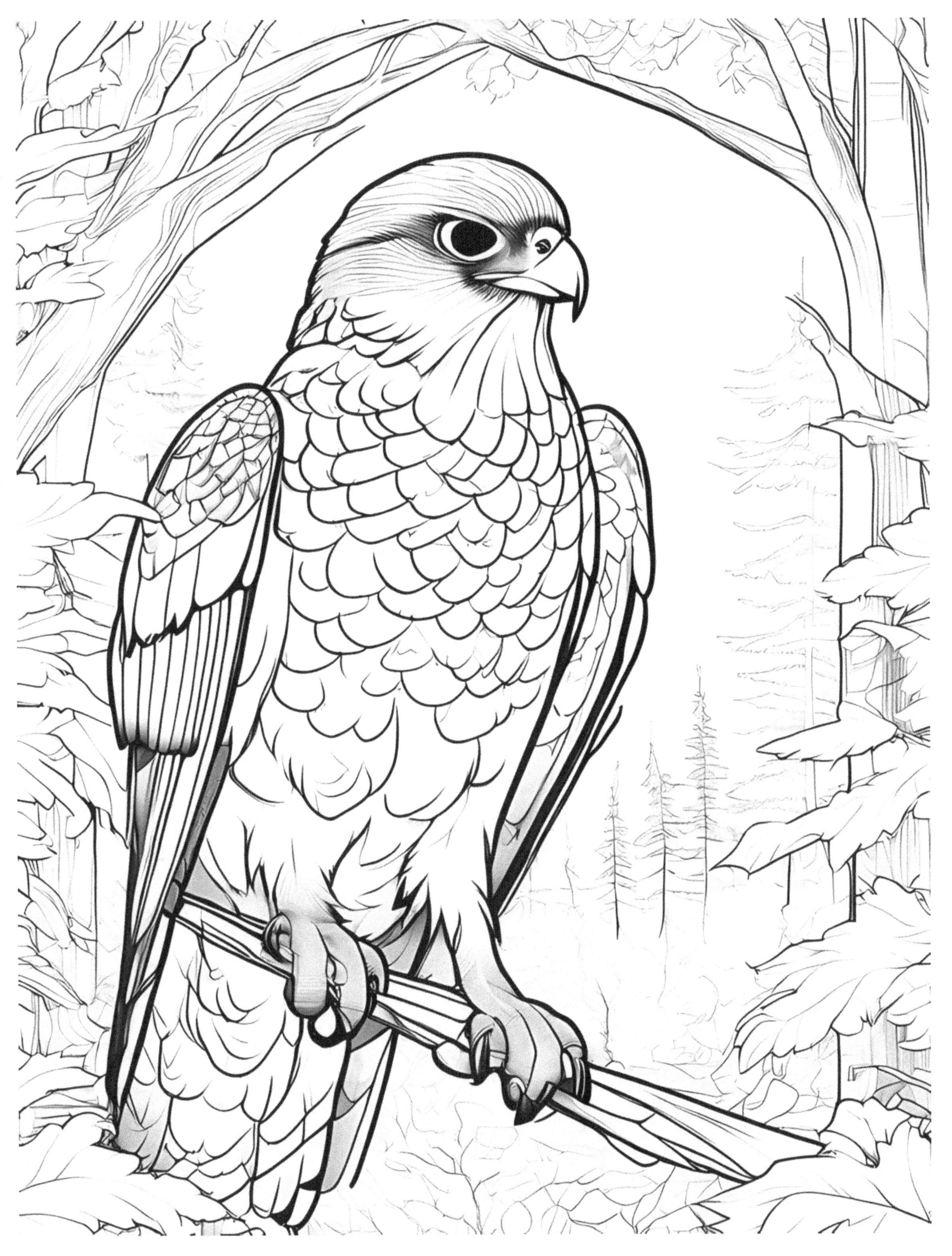

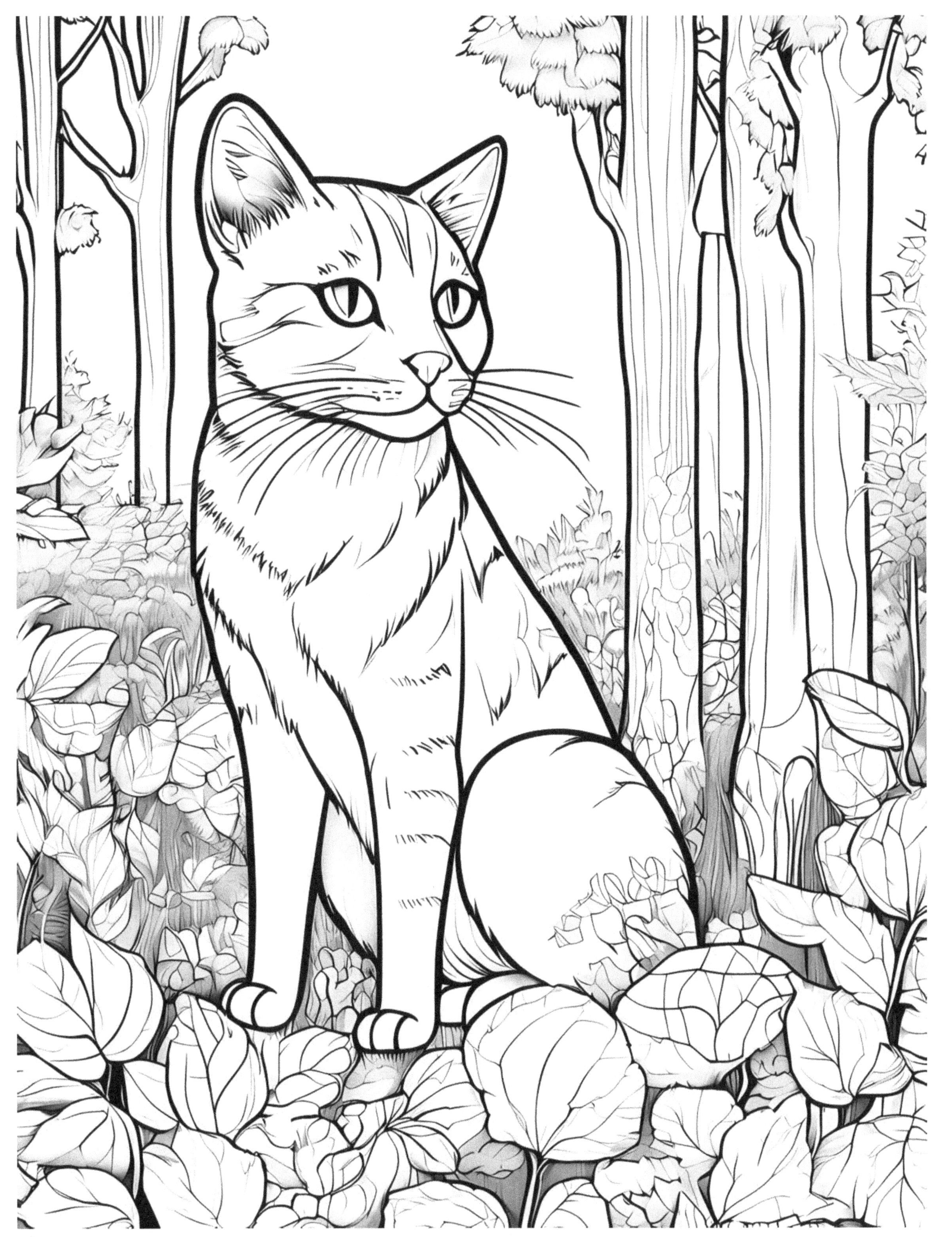